From the Heart of the Applegate

Essays, Poems, and Short
Fiction by Applegate Writers

PUBLISHED BY
Applegate Valley Community Newspaper, Inc.
dba *Applegater* Newsmagazine
Applegate Valley, Oregon

ISBN-13: 978-0-692-60406-9 (Applegate Valley
        Community Newspaper, Inc.)
ISBN-10: 0692604065

Applegate Valley Community Newspaper, Inc.
PO Box 14
Jacksonville, OR 97530
www.applegater.org
gater@applegater.org

Acknowledgements

Chris Bratt for the idea for this book.

The Board of Directors of the *Applegater*
for their support of this project.

Barbara Holiday for editing and
commandeering the project.

Diana Coogle for editing.

The selection committee, comprised of Diana Coogle,
Barbara Holiday, John Taylor,
Richard Williams, and Linda Yates.

All the writers who submitted pieces.
We wish we could have included them all.

TABLE OF CONTENTS

POETRY

Author Biographies

Introduction

It takes only two things to be a writer—a writing tool, of personal choice, and inspiration, which the Applegate provides in abundance. The beauty of our surroundings— snow on Grayback, golden big-leaf maple trees, lambs gamboling in green pastures, the Applegate River at Cantrall Buckley Park, rain drumming outside while we sit cozy by a fire in the stove—all that beauty inspires us to observe with our senses as well as with the prodding intellect of our minds and memories. Then, if we are writers, we take up that writing tool and begin.

With that rich beginning come the poems, stories, and recorded thoughts of Applegate writers. Many of these writers are represented in these pages, but, as it turned out, the selections committee received more good writing than they were able to include. The thirty-six poets, short story writers, and essayists in this anthology are representative of the others.

By submission requirements, the writers all live in the Applegate, defined as the area served by the *Applegater* (generally, from Jacksonville to Wilderville and parts of Grants Pass). They live in the mountains and in the valley. They are women and men (though the ethnic diversity is slim, representative as it is of the general population). They range in age from eighteen to ninety-four. They are award-winning writers and put-it-in-the-journal writers. Some have lived in the Applegate for decades; others have been here only a few years. Some of the pieces are humorous (**Connie Fowler, J.D. Rogers**); some take a serious tone (**Kirsten K. Shockey, Jane Robin**); some are dark (**Tressi Innana Albee**), some light

(**Morgan Jordan**); some speak widely (**Thalia Truesdell**); some come from spiritual depths (**John Richard Sack**); some are rooted in the earth (**Haley Morgan May**). Applegate writers write about family they love (**Christin Lore Weber**) and strangers they meet (**Alice Gelston Migliore**), about neighbors (**Paul Tipton**) and new relationships (**Beate Foit**). They write about pets (**Marilyn Terry**) and cars (**Dolores Durando**), trees (**Gay Bradshaw**) and birds (**Joan Peterson**), rain (**Joy La Spina**) and snow (**Linda Kappen**). They write about their childhoods (**Seth Kaplan**) and about corpses of ancient people (**Alice Gelston Migliore**), about things as small as tadpoles (**Christina Strelova**) and as grand as the universe (**Greeley Wells**), about life and death (**Laurie Easter, Heather Murphy**), love and grief (**Kayleigh B. McKey**), adventures big (**J.D. Rogers**) and small (**Marina Walker**). They write personal stories (**Lily Myers Kaplan, Stew Towle**), thoughtful reflections (**Anna Elkins, Carol Hoon**), passionate outcries (**H. Ní Aódagaín**), whimsical insights (**Diana Coogle**). And although some of these pieces are set in the Applegate (**Barbara Summerhawk, Ty Thomas Luckman**) and some in distant places (**Lisa E. Baldwin**'s poem about the desert; **Chris Bratt** on Orcas Island; **Tressi Innana Albee**'s essay, set in Kenya), the writers all share a love for this place that is reflected in the biographies following the entries.

The inspiration of living in the Applegate, it seems, is good for writers. Open these pages and see how true that is.

Diana Coogle

Chair, *Applegater* Board of Directors

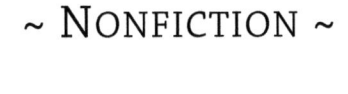

~ NONFICTION ~

Leila

Tressi Innana Albee

I met Leila at the Fondu Wehu guesthouse on the coast of the Indian Ocean in the small town of Malindi, where I was on a welcome break from the political upheaval in Nairobi. When Leila arrived, my back stiffened. I could actually feel her presence, like an ancient Somali tribal queen. She was tall, long-necked and high cheekboned with skin as smooth and dark as ebony.

From the moment we met, Leila and I spoke the language of sisterhood, like a secret dialect embedded in our DNA. We spent the next several weeks as steady companions sharing bits of our lives like tasty morsels of chocolate. Over the next week Leila and I played on the beach, and we embarked on the task of finding the most authentic Swahili food we could find in Malindi. We visited graveyards and art galleries and played with the curious kids on the beach. We giggled like little girls when we caught a glimpse of the prostitutes coming on to the *wazungu* tourists.

About a week into our stay at the breezy, thatch-roofed guesthouse, I took a phone call for Leila, who was out being romanced at the beach by her American boyfriend. Through the choppy telephone connection, I discovered that Leila's father had just died suddenly. It became my undertaking to bring this epic news to Leila when she returned from her love frolic. I had already dined on the morsels of Leila's story; I knew she and her family were refugees from Somalia because the United States was waging a secret war in her homeland. I knew she shared a deep love with an American man and this enraged her father. As I held Leila through the days of tears, grief, and confusion, our bond was forged everlasting.

During those days Leila and I shared an intimacy that I had never known before. She spent hours in my arms grieving as the women in her lineage have done for eons—full-bodied grief, stream of consciousness storytelling, and rivers of tears. In our sheltered amity, Leila shared stories of her childhood with me. I learned that she was circumcised in the way her tribal custom requires. At the age of five, Leila, along with all the other girls her age, was taken in the night from her safe bed to the schoolhouse. I imagined the walls that once held the teachings of children, now holding their wails of agony as the painful and bloody operation unfolded long into the night. The cutting was followed by weeks of recovery that ended girlhood definitively.

The custom of Leila's tribe was not only to remove the clitoris, but also to remove the inner labia and sew the outer labia closed, leaving only a small opening through which to urinate and menstruate. Leila explained that after the frightening abduction and the intrusive operation, all the girls lay on their sides for weeks with their legs tied together so that the passageway of purity would fuse closed and the aching wounds could heal. Leila and the other girls were cared for and brought through their initiation by the caring hands and loving words of the elder women of her tribe, the ancient wisdom of womanhood spilling from one generation to the next just as it had since the beginning of memory. Leila casually explained that this kind of circumcision keeps the woman safe from men's desire and, more importantly, pure for her husband. The surprising theme of Leila's story was that the ceremony of female circumcision was precisely what made her a woman.

If I understood correctly, Leila was professing that she had her quintessentially female parts removed and remodeled and that that is what made her a woman. My own belief that there is a powerful and intimate connection between my organic female body and my notion of womanhood was shattered. Though Leila's initiation into womanhood seemed brutal from my perspective, she thought my lack of any formal initiation was equally devastating. During the weeks of recovery the young initiates were enlightened about what it meant to be a woman, how to be a good wife, the value of modesty, the art of sisterhood, the mysteries of menstruation and sexuality, and the treasured secrets the women held about childbirth and mothering.

Leila was correct in her assessment that I lacked initiation. When I was thirteen years old, there was an initiation ceremony performed by the crone-aged women of our Unitarian Universalist congregation. The ceremony was meant to welcome us to womanhood. We gathered in one of the holy places of my childhood, the statuary garden, where the statues of four beautiful and powerful, nude African-

American women forged of rough iron were erected in a small pool with steppingstones. The statues represent the artist's interpretation of the adult version of the four little girls killed in the Birmingham, Alabama, church bombing in 1963. These feminine icons, four women, represent the four directions, or the aspects of freedom, liberation, sacrifice, and peace. At each direction we were offered a trinket: a black stone, a white feather, blood red flowers, and wise words to mark our transformation from girlhood to womanhood. But there was something missing in this tradition. It lacked roots that connected us to a personal lineage and tribal tradition. I cannot say with the same assurance that Leila shared that the ceremony marked my definitive passage into womanhood. Did it mean I was not a woman? What does it mean to be a woman? I began to see womanhood in more subtle tones than ever before.

I came to understand womanhood as the language of sisterhood that both Leila and I spoke fluently and effortlessly. Womanhood was the instinctual comfort I offered to Leila in her grief, though I had yet to be in grief's merciless grip myself. Womanhood was the outpouring of compassion I felt when I wondered if Leila and her initiated sisters would ever know the joy of female sexual pleasure. I came to understand womanhood as a potent mixture of tenderness, compassion, and intuition. This awareness made me acutely mindful that these qualities seem to be in short supply on a global scale. Leila's story sent me searching for my own initiation into womanhood, with the hope that I might initiate others and bring more balance to our world, one initiated woman at a time.

Still Life

Gay Bradshaw

Summer has passed her crown to fall. The shift has been gentle, unlike the arguments that entangle winter and spring. Nonetheless, summer shows last-minute reluctance, as we all do, happy to feel the edge of heat give way to the frisson of autumn nights, but saddened by her exit. In this season I enter into negotiations with the aged crabapple tree standing imperturbable on the graceful shoulder of a grassy hill.

The air has quickened, and the turkeys, skunks, and squirrels have focused their efforts to gather the season's last banquet. (There is no shortfall like the meanness of winter). Acorns bounce down from heaven, and grasshoppers dance long-legged in golden fields. All has prospered from a tender summer and the kindness of a rainy spring. But now we are hastening with a sense of finitude.

Every evening, I walk out to the crabapple tree and gaze across the stretch of field to the pensive dark mountains. Every evening, the deer circle me in what has become a decades' old ritual—the shaking of the tree.

The tree and I have aged. Her boughs and my limbs have less spring. We have grown quiet in the wisdom that comes with the cycles of love and loss. We play our game as always —she, reticent to give over her gold and reds, and I, insistent that the time to share has come.

The easy fruit is gone, most of it ravaged clean by the teeth of passing cows. She reminds me: "You have already spent some of my gold." It is true. When the apples were newly fresh and bright, I begged and wheedled for an early crop, to give the wandering cows.

Their gaze is different from the deer's, intense with foreknowledge. As soon as the hint of autumn comes, the cows are coaxed—no, coerced—into waiting trucks. None go easy. They bay and bellow, protesting the blackness of death that awaits at the slaughterhouse.

The cows are gone. The deer remain. They are more confident. Perhaps their composure draws from hope. They, at least, may imagine a fate other than the inevitable one meted out to the cows. Year after year, century after century, millennium after millennium, that knowledge passes from cow and bull to calf. The horror is bred into the marrow of their bones.

And now, the deer share a similar story. They still carry the strains of legends before the fall, the fall of the year, the fall of the buck, and the fall of the does and fawns who buckle to the ground with the empty lust of human hearts. They have changed. I have changed.

Together, the crabapple tree and I sit in the lonesome dusk. The slaughter is upon us. We wait, silent, comforted only by the fact there is still life.

Climbing Chirripó

Diana Coogle

This piece is from a forthcoming book, Wisdom of the Heart, *by Diana Coogle (essays) and Barbara Kostal (paintings). Each painting has an accompanying essay written in response to it. This essay was written in response to the painting titled "Spiritus."*

At 12,529 feet (3,819 meters) Chirripó is Costa Rica's highest mountain. On the first day of a planned three-day trek up the mountain, my friend Tom and I hiked for seven and a half hours, first through tropical jungle vegetation with occasional flowers and copious bird whistles, calls, warblings, and songs, then up a very steep trail, out of the jungle into the páramo and through oak forests, both living and burned. Signs marked our ascent kilometer by kilometer: 1, The Monkeys. 2, The Machine's Cemetery Ridge. (Kilometer 3 was missing a sign.) 4, The Resplendent Quetzal, whose habitat we were crossing. 5, The Oaks. 6, The Chlorophonia (a bird with a green song, perhaps?). 7, Beautiful Plain. 8, Water's Climb.

Steeper and steeper. Wind. Rocks. Kilometer 9, Old Man's Beard. 10, The Bamboo. 11, The Burns. 12, Without Faith Mountain ("I have no faith I'll make it to the top"?).

Ceanothus, in bloom at 11,000 feet! No more birds. Kilometer 12, The Flowers (not many in August). 13, The Repentants ("I repent I ever started this climb"?). Finally, kilometer 14, El Ultimo Paso, The Last Step—or almost. Half a kilometer farther, we reached a climber's refuge, the *albergue.* The weather was cold and viciously windy. The showers were ice cold.

At eight o'clock the next morning, we started for the peak, three and a half kilometers away. After half a kilometer, Tom, suffering from altitude sickness, returned to the *albergue.* I continued alone through a beautifully stark landscape. The fog thickened as the trail gained altitude. The last ascent rose straight up a narrowing stone peak, a bone of the earth towering vertically into the air. At last I broke through to the summit, a small flat bit of earth and rock. The sides of the mountain dropped sheer to the earth below. This stone column, this upright bone of the earth, had thrust me, except for my earthbound feet, into air, but it was an air heavily laden with moisture. I am told there is a magnificent view from the top of Chirripó, that half of Costa Rica can be seen and, on good days, both the Pacific and Atlantic oceans, but I saw only fog, twisting like cyclones in the cold wind.

It is only the infinity of air that makes a blue sky. Fog makes a sky finite. Once, years ago, walking through the woods behind a neighbor's house, I saw my four-year-old son and a friend of his sitting on the edge of the front porch. The friend was saying, "You know, there's really no such thing as a sky. It's all air—blue air." The two little boys sat there, not talking, swinging their legs, contemplating the vastness of air, of *spiritus,* that which we breathe, which gives us life: blue air. Or, in the case of Chirripó on this particular day, gray air.

For fifteen minutes on Chirripó, I was the highest person in Costa Rica. Then I succumbed to the cold and descended.

When I walked into the *albergue* just at noon, Tom was packing his gear. "Well," he said, without further preamble, "are you ready to hike down the mountain?"

A little astonished at not being asked about my tremendous achievement—or for my opinion about a change of plans—I blurted, "I *would* like to rest a minute." But Tom was ready to leave, so we did, wisely, as it turned out, because by the time we reached our hotel at the trailhead, we were hiking in the dark. Tom, who had slipped on the steep, muddy parts of the trail and had fallen three or four times, was so delirious with fatigue that when we met in front of the hotel before dinner, he didn't recognize me and spoke to me as to a stranger. As for me, I had been hiking for ten hours straight with no more than a few minutes of rest every now and then. I had climbed a little over two miles to a mountain peak and then descended 11,286 feet in eleven miles. I was so tired I had to force my body to walk the few yards to the restaurant. But if tiredness was weighing my body down, elation was elevating my spirit. I had made the pilgrimage to what is called, and surely is, the magical destination of Chirripó. I had lived for fifteen minutes in complete *spiritus*. I was foot-weary and heart-happy.

Saving the Calf

Connie Fowler

"As I was out walkin' one mornin' for pleasure / In tee shirt and shorts as often I do. Yippee Ty Yi Yo..."

This story started out as a parody on that old cowboy song, but somehow it just never worked out that way. I couldn't even write it at all for several years, but finally the time was right.

The hot July sun lazed on the horizon as I started out on my summer evening walk. It was still plenty warm, but I felt almost cool in pink tee shirt, shorts, and my good running shoes. While the attire might seem inappropriate for a rancher's wife, it suits me when it is hot and I'm not ranchin'.

We ran a herd of commercial mother cows, and I glanced up the hill where they grazed contentedly. I knew one old cow was close to calving, and I thought I saw her munching grass with the rest. Good, nothing to worry about, I thought, and I started walking briskly in the field along the little river that tumbles the length of our property.

Not too far along the way I thought I heard something, and I slid to a stop, listening. "What the heck was that?" I said out loud. "Maaaaaaahhhh." Impossible. It sounded like a baby calf bawl coming from the river. No way a calf could be in the river. Besides, I saw that cow up on the hill, didn't I? "Maaaaaaahhhh." There it was again. My heart sank.

Frantic, I looked around for a way to get down to the river. Since a tangle of blackberries around an old fence formed a barrier along its bank, I backtracked looking for a hole. Finding one several yards back, I climbed down. I couldn't believe my eyes. There he was, a very big red and white calf, knee deep in the water and bawling his little head off. How on earth did he get there, and how in the name of Roy Rogers was I going to get him out?

Panic set in. I ran back to the house as fast as I could to get a rope and put on my old shoes. No time to change clothes. Who knew what the little bovine might do to himself trying to get out of the river.

My husband was somewhere up the road doing some irrigating, so there was no point in yelling for help. No cell phones. No neighbors close. I'd have to cowgirl up and figure out how to get the critter to his mama, who apparently gave up on him and went back to the herd. She definitely wouldn't make Mother of the Year.

Now, I know stuff and things about cattle, and the one thing I knew for sure was that you can't lead a calf or push one either. Time being of the essence, and with no better plan, I decided to put the lariat rope around his girth and, by pushing and pulling, get him up through a small opening in the berry barrier I saw a ways up river.

So, I pulled and he balked, and I pushed and he dug his little hooves in. He jumped forward, and I fell down. I pushed, and he fell down. Wrestling and thrashing, we made little progress. Once or twice we both went under in a deeper hole in the otherwise shallow summer stream. Convinced that the sorry little critter would now surely die of mechanical pneumonia, I screamed at him, "You might die later, but I am going to get you out of this river alive if it kills me."

In a time frame that seemed like forever, the calf and I bumped along, inches at a time, in total opposition until we finally reached the only possible way out. "Can't you realize I'm trying to help you, you stubborn animal?" I gasped. Even with the cool water, the heat and exertion would soon take its toll on both of us.

I tried to drag the calf, 70-plus pounds, up the steep five-foot bank through the blackberries and fence, but he slipped out of my rope and fell backwards into the river. Terrified he would drown for sure, I decided to see if I could push him up. With what must have been supernatural strength, I finally got him through the brambles, and with one final, muscle-taxing effort, I pushed him under the barbed-wire fence on to solid ground.

By now the hungry baby thought I was mom and eagerly sucked my finger as I bent over trying to catch my breath. Limping, panting, with baby calf attached to my finger, I started slowly up the field toward the house.

Just then, husband Ben and mama cow both spotted us at the same time. Ben started yelling, "Get out of the way! Get out of the way!" I thought he was worried the cow would hurt me. Wrong. "Get out of the way so the cow can bond with the calf!" he kept yelling even though the calf saw his mom and figured her swollen udder presented a better chance for a meal than my index finger.

Gasping and gulping for air, I finally reached Ben. Still making sure the mom and baby joined up, he just didn't notice my red, mud-smeared face, blackberry briars sticking out all over my bird-nest hair, multiple scratches on my arms, wet and muddy shoes, once-pink shirt and shorts.

Between breaths, I tried to explain my plight, hoping for a shred of sympathy. When none came as Ben continued to watch the pair ambling up the hill, I staggered to the house steaming with anger mixed with exhaustion. Once in the house, I took a warm bath, swallowed four ibuprofen tablets, and went to bed.

Now, I could have stayed mad, but I understood how important cow-calf bonding is along with that first all-important colostrum-loaded milk. The last thing either of us wanted to do was raise the calf on a bottle. So I cowgirled up again, and when I really thought about it, no one but the calf and I knew the true story. No matter how many adjectives and adverbs I interjected. No matter how much arm waving and no matter how many cuts and bruises showed, nothing short of a video (or now a GoPro) would do the story justice. Like now.

So, it was just one of those "ya had to be there" events. I tried telling the story now and then, but most people just shook their heads or said, "Wow, that must have been something."

The calf? The whole ordeal didn't phase him one bit. He grew up big and strong. Of course I don't know what he told his mom and the rest of the herd, but I can't help but think his mama sympathized with his near miss with death. For me? No thanks from her, either.

Since the whole thing was so traumatic, I didn't see any humor in it (really? you say) so I just couldn't write about it for several years. Until now. Like I said, I wanted to write a song, but the only one that came to mind was, "Nobody Knows the Trouble I've Seen."

The Crowning

Lily Myers Kaplan

The first time I met the great Goddess Demeter was in the mid 1970s. I was in my twenties. It was the first day of spring. The sky pressed down with grey winds, and flurries of snow mixed with icy rain. Frank, the elder among my rag-tag crew of growers, landscapers, and counselors—horticulture therapists, all—called us together for a small ceremony welcoming the new season.

We gathered in a steam-fogged greenhouse, standing on pebbly sand in muddy boots and plaid flannel shirts tucked into thick corduroy pants and surrounded by dank mossy undergrowth and long beds empty of potted plants. A dusky, late-afternoon sunlight filtered through soil-encrusted panes of wavy glass. We raised glasses of beer clutched in bruised and blistered hands, our dirty fingernails an ode to our proud profession in which hands sank into dark, rich soil and soaked in juicy green chlorophyll.

With our sacred elixir held high, Frank intoned the mythical story of the ancient Greeks describing the passage of winter into spring. He told us of the deep bond between two Goddesses—a mother and daughter—named Demeter and Persephone, whose tale described vibrant earth turned into fallow land and back again. Falling into a sing-song cadence Frank intoned,

"In her wild innocence the maiden Persephone collected narcissus in a sunlit meadow, out of sight of her mother, Demeter. Suddenly the earth cracked open. Hades, King of the Underworld, burst forth on a gleaming chariot pulled by two black stallions. Abducting Persephone in one swoop, he returned to the earthy den from which he rose. The ground closed its doors behind him.

"Demeter wandered through forest and cornfield, searching, though Persephone was nowhere to be found. Filled with grief, Demeter wailed. She howled. And then she retreated. Demeter—the Goddess of the Grain and the Giver of Life—recoiled from the world. Grain began to wither. Without Demeter's motherly presence winter was laid upon the earth.

"Winter, with its long, dark nights, sapped the world of its strength. Food became scarce. Humanity suffered. People cried out until Zeus, King of all the Gods and Goddesses, became weary of their weeping. He commanded Hades to release Persephone. Hallelujah!

"Mother and daughter were reunited, and Demeter poured life into the earth once more. Grain was restored and a new cycle of growth—spring—began. Because Persephone had eaten three juicy red pomegranate seeds in the Underworld, she had married her soul to Hades. The seeds within her belly sealed her fate: she would return to the Underworld for three months each year. Winter would come again as a time of hibernation and seed-renewal, and it would always be followed by spring, a time of rebirth.

"Today, let us welcome Persephone back! Let us greet her and celebrate this first day of spring with joy, inviting the spirit of renewed growth into our humble greenhouses. May abundance reign here again!"

With that we poured our grainy fermented brew into the earth as a prayer for a bountiful season. That was my first ceremonial ritual outside the Jewish tradition of my birth—and the first of my true religion. We had entered into the rites of spring as growers of plants and supporters of souls. As I watched the earth drink the ale at our feet, I thought, *I'm home.*

To say that our ritual celebration of Persephone and Demeter created the beauty that followed would be naive. But after digging up buried terracotta pots planted with bulbs of hyacinth, narcissus, and tulips from beneath their icy blanket of snow and watching long-empty flower beds burst with green sprouts peeking from bare dirt, I wondered at the miracle of rebirth. Withered tubers had resurrected into a greenhouse of color before my eyes. Purple hyacinths, sweet as honeysuckle, shouted their thick sugary scent in all directions. The perky yellow happiness of daffodils cheered my spirits, and passionate red tulips opened my heart.

But to say that this rich and vibrant shared ceremony awakened my sense of partnership with the cycles of life and that my human consciousness tapped into the wider and wilder mysteries of an archetypal, mythical world is truer still. Though I didn't know it then, this myth would guide me throughout my life.

In my thirties I traveled gypsy-like among earth-centered cultures, living close to the earth and experiencing the cycles firsthand. I felt my own blood rise in wild sexual exploits each spring. Then I cozied into a slower rhythm each fall with long introspective walks over crunching leaves in crisp sweater-wearing air. I came to know—in the deepest way of knowing —that my animal body is made of the same matter as the earth. Watching the sun move from the northern to the southern sky, I could feel the planet rotating through space. I realized that the most minute micro-cell within a cell within a cell within my body is spinning in much the same pattern as the macro larger-than-conceivable solar system. I had discovered what indigenous people know from an early age—that life continues in a never-ending cycle of seasons upon seasons upon seasons—a mysterious spiral.

With that revelation came a deepened trust in my own cycles. I understood that no matter how dark the days of my outer world or how long the nights of my inner one, Persephone would rise again. Spring—a rebirth on the land and within my inner landscape—would always return.

In my forties I moved to California, where I sought a master's degree in culture and spirituality and revisited the myth as part of my studies. That's when I realized that Persephone's transformation in the Underworld, from young maiden to grown woman, was much like my own forged path of leaving my east coast home to live thousands of miles from family. And, like Persephone, I found a soul-partner with whom I could spend the rest of my life—Seth—and we were married. Marriage changed me—I not only adopted a new name, but I embraced a whole new identity. I'd been initiated.

Ancient storytellers knew that the process of initiation is hidden, much like the transformation of seeds, deep in the earth, during the winter. I found out that Frank's version, told in the humid glass greenhouse, wasn't the whole picture. Twenty years after our first introduction, I met the great Goddess Demeter again, and her more complex story goes like this:

During Demeter's search for Persephone she searched so long and grieved so hard that her cloak became tattered. Once vibrant, Demeter lost her Goddess glow as she dragged herself from forest to town, eventually coming to a small village,

Eleusis, where she collapsed beside a well. It was tended by young women who began combing, braiding and placing flowers into Demeter's hair while rubbing aromatic herbs into her skin and giving her sips of water until she surrendered into their care and slowly revived.

When the Goddess Baubo, a giant, bawdy, dancing vulva, appeared, lewdly thrusting hips as she told a series of off-color jokes, Demeter cracked a smile—just as Eleusis's Lady of the Manor arrived. Finding this smiling, apparently gentle washer-woman, the Lady offered Demeter a job nursing her newborn son. Demeter became a nanny. As Demeter cared for the young boy, she found a new purpose, secretly placing him into the burning flames at the hearth each night, giving him immortality.

When the Lady arrived unexpectedly one night and saw her son engulfed in flames, she shrieked and grabbed him from the fire. Demeter threw off her torn grey cloak, gathered into her full height, and revealed her true identity, saying, "I am the Great Demeter: Goddess of the Grain!" At this very moment Persephone ate three pomegranate seeds, married Hades, and became Queen of the Underworld.

Mother and Daughter were reunited in a grand celebration, and the town Eleusis built them a Temple. Demeter and Persephone became known throughout all the lands as the Keepers of the Elysian Mysteries, a secret sect of Priests and Priestesses devoted to the cycles of transformation.

The Great Goddess Demeter showed me that death is a necessary part of life, that the biblical phrase "walking through the Valley of Death" is about the process of becoming whole. Shedding the grey cloak of what no longer felt true to my Self became my path. I said yes to death. Soon enough I was in a full-blown winter—the tumultuous journey all women experience as we age and our bodies are abducted a second time. As my estrogen faded and belly softened, I spent night after night deep in sweat, tossing off covers, only to pull them back minutes later, shivering. Clammy, I lay awake wondering just how long this Middle Passage would go on. It was a real midlife crisis, with attendant ponderings on what I was really supposed to be doing with my life. I started revisiting everything. As I swore off turtlenecks forever and kept the window open at night—in all seasons—I found the courage to accept this descent into a winter of my soul.

I was in my late fifties when, losing both parents, I came face to face with literal death. But beyond that, when my sister, Lois, died, I came into the most profound state of unknowing I'd experienced to date. Who would I be in a world without a Lois in it? I had no idea. For months all I did was clean closets, then the garage. One day, tired after a thousand trips to Goodwill with boxes of stuff, I collaged a small box—a tiny casket. Filled with small items, symbols of all that I was no more, I put a stamp—a heart—on the casket and addressed it, "To the Underworld." Inserting a letter to Queen Persephone, I asked for help through this dark time, saying, "I am on the precipice of death—the death of each of the roles of my life. Endings are new beginnings, as I know, yet for a new beginning to emerge, I need to accept the losses. Please help me."

I took the casket on a pilgrimage through the Sierra. I gazed at snowcapped mountains and tumbling waterfalls and finally sat beside a gurgling creek. I took a deep breath, hugged that tiny sarcophagus to my chest, and with all my love, tossed it into cold rushing waters. Right then and there, as I watched it sink out of sight, I promised myself that Lois's death, and my grief, would not be without meaning. That night I had a powerful, reassuring dream…

Mom, Dad and Lois stand ceremonially before me in shimmering, vibrant spirit bodies. Mom is in front, holding up a diamond-studded tiara that she places on my head, saying, "It is up to you to carry on the matriarchal lineage." Lois steps forward, hands me a sheaf of files, and says, "It's up to you to carry on my work." Dad says, simply, "I am proud of you." As the headdress melts into the top of my head—my crown-chakra—I accept Lo's papers. I wake up with tears running down my cheeks.

It felt momentous, as if I'd experienced a visitation. Soon I began to write. The writing healed me. And as I turned sixty, my book, a memoir of love and loss entwined with Lo's ever-present reminder that Love is all that matters, was published. I found meaning in losing Lois, but beyond that, I found my voice. Like Demeter, I tossed off the grey cloak of sorrow to find that my mother's crowning had taken root. I had stepped into the power of my maternal lineage and my inner wise woman. I had un-layered until all that was left was my Self.

Taking the book on the road, I passed through Ashland. I'm sure it was my sister's voice that I heard as I walked down Siskiyou Boulevard, headed to Morning Glory for breakfast. Exuberant, deeply satisfied, filled with my true Self, I spread my arms wide, took a deep breath, then heard the words, "This place smells like home." It was the exact phrase I'd said to Lo more than thirty years before as we set foot for the first time in Oakland, California. Ten years later I moved there, where I lived and loved for nearly twenty-three years.

Stepping off the train with Lois back in 1982, I'd been referring to our shared homeland of Baltimore, Maryland, and the salty scent of the Chesapeake Bay. In Oakland, the San Francisco Bay wafted the familiar trace of sea and sand. But in Ashland there is no salty ocean to drift an accustomed salt-water scent into my heart. Still, it came. Hearing those words again, I knew, with an abiding trust, that a moving van was in my future.

I have just celebrated the fifth anniversary of Lois's death and my first spring in Applegate Valley, where I root into the tough clay-red earth. I mourn that Lois, a birder extraordinaire, is not here to watch the acorn woodpeckers feed their young or listen to the distant owl in the late-late night and tell me its truest name. I miss her, sometimes in a raw, unspeakable way, other times with a sweet melancholy, and I wish I could hug her angular, soft-skinned body. Though I cannot hear them, her whispers into the ears of my heart offer comfort: she is not far away.

Seth and I looked for a home in walkable Ashland, but sadly, no place there rang true. Disappointed, we rambled to Jacksonville, and I found myself smitten. As we looked more actively, the whispers—more like a vortex I could not resist— drew us further. We began walking on oak savannah and in madrone-rich forest. As we wandered on more acres than we'd ever dreamed of, a memory grabbed me, a long-carried image of my elder-Self. In my dreamy vision I am living in a small hut at the edge of a rural village. Rafters are hung with pungent sage, interlaced with bundles of sweet rose, lavender, and yarrow. Elder-Lily is peacefully rocking in her bent-willow rocker, receiving villagers who come with trade, seeking council. The reciprocity gives great solace, in both directions. I know myself as just one small piece of this big-hearted community, an interrelated ecosystem of people and place.

While not yet old, but having entered the third chapter of my life, I have arrived at the well, from which I drink deeply, and have tossed off my grey cloak, standing at my full height, claiming my true heritage. Having come all the way through the Middle Passage, I carry out the tasks of my ancestral lineage and, like Demeter, have become a woman-unto-herself. I have found my homeland, both within and outside me. My hut is real; it is a Temple from which I write and receive stories, enacting the secret mysteries of transformation. I am often found there, sitting in Lo's bentwood rocker, sometimes writing, other times in counsel with those who seek it, always bringing my dream to life. Who I am no longer needs defining. I am, finally, just me. Wholeheartedly, whole.

A Bit of Earth

Haley Morgan May

Our grandmother, whose belly was a star, begat the elements of mother earth, the dust from which all life arose. For four and a half billion years, gravity has been the same as it was in the beginning, drawing earth's children to its center from birth to death. Dust to dust. As Neil deGrasse Tyson puts it in the hit television series *Cosmos*, "Earth pulls on us. Our lives are a relentless struggle with gravity. From our first efforts to stand to our final surrender, we are struggling to overcome the Earth's pull. We are born, live, and die in a force field, one that is almost as old as the universe itself, 13.8 billion years."

We live in a prison we cannot escape.

Earth pulls on us. Across the world, we kneel, press our foreheads to the ground. We kiss terra firma with gratitude after weeks at sea. Mineral pools bubbling from the planet's core draw us to their soothing waters, heal our tired bodies. Each night, we upend our centers of gravity and sleep, momentarily convinced to stop resisting.

But as long as earth pulls on us, we pull on her. Gravity attracts all bodies to one another. When our foreheads bow into the dirt, two global force fields meet in worship. The force field of a human head draws the planet towards itself. We pull on the earth. At 9.81 meters per second squared, earth rises to meet our lips, obeying the unbreakable laws of nature. She dutifully slips her immense hands beneath our tired backs as we snore, each breath taken in relativity to her mass.

We pull on the earth, digging, weeding, planting trees that defy gravity's presence. When the force fields of humans and earth collide, soils turn, roses stretch to the heavens, waves of grain bend in the breeze and then reach again for the sky. Trees bulge with fruit that then falls on the heads of puzzled physicists. A small portion of the sphere becomes our own as we coax up artichokes, hollyhocks, grapes: a garden, a place to co-create and to observe inevitable death.

In *The Secret Garden*, by Frances Hodgson Burnett, a sickly and rejected girl, Mary, is summoned by her uncle, the wealthy Lord Craven of Yorkshire. As her new guardian, who is unable to give her any real attention or time, he asks her:

"Is there anything you want? Do you want toys, books, dolls?"

"Might I," quavers Mary, "might I have a bit of earth?"

"Earth!" he repeats. "What do you mean?"

"To plant seeds in—to make things grow—to see them come alive," Mary falters.

Her uncle instructs her to take what she wishes, from anywhere, and says good-bye. Unwittingly, he gifts her the Secret Garden, the heart and soul of the late Mrs. Craven, her mother's sister. Mary's aunt was killed by a falling branch in the very same garden, that bit of earth that was her life and death.

With the door locked and the key buried, the Secret Garden lay dormant, unloved, sickly, forgotten, not unlike poor Mary. But the laws of nature are constant. Life cycles continue from death to rebirth. The garden is tended by Mary, the act of which, in turn, brings her to life. In the Broadway musical, Lord Craven sings,

She should have a pony, gallop 'cross the moor
She should have a doll's house with a hundred
    rooms per floor

Why can't she ask for a treasure? Something that
    money can buy
That won't die, When I'd give her the world, she
    asks instead for some earth
She'll grow to love
The tender roses, lilies fair, the iris tall
And then in fall, her bit of earth
Will freeze and kill them all.

Once we accept that change is inevitable, we realize there is no fixed place in the cosmos. All of nature is in motion. Earth pulls on us, we pull on the earth, seasons generate sprouts and fruit, currents of moisture and wind lay ruin to crops, we struggle on tiny feet to stand, we get old, we fall. But we don't let gravity get us down. We pull on the earth as it hurtles through space.

Tyson reminds us that even when we are standing still, listening to the birds, "earth is turning at more than 1,600 kilometers per hour while it orbits the Sun at more than 100,000 kilometers per hour. And the Sun is moving through the galaxy at a half a million miles per hour. And the Milky Way is moving through the universe at nearly one and a half million miles an hour." As we walk through deserts, drive across swamps, plant beds of onions, the ground is moving.

When stars of a certain mass die and their fuel begins to run out, they become black holes, bending space-time. Not even light can escape their incredible gravitational pull. It is thought that at the center of most galaxies, supermassive black holes exist, absorbing stars and merging with other black holes.

When our sun is finally sucked in and becomes timeless and spaceless, perhaps it emerges on the other side in a parallel universe, where life doesn't end, time and space are constant, light doesn't bend, and gravity barely has a grip. We float free, wandering and wondering whether another kind of life exists beyond us, a life where gardens grow and heal humans and the humans revitalize a bit of earth, where we are the makers of change rather than those who suffer from it. We pull on the earth, and the earth pulls on us. All is well and in balance forever in our secret garden.

When Heroes Die

H. Ní Aódagaín

"How are you?" I ask loudly, frustrated by the static weaving itself through the phone.

"I'm okay." A pause. "She leaves tomorrow, and I guess once she's gone, I'll start dating."

For a while now, Marcus and his wife of twenty-five years have been in dialogue about her desire to be in a polyamorous relationship. At first, he was vehemently opposed, but after three years in which she has insisted that a polyamorous relationship is what she needs, he has become resigned. He's not willing to divorce her, as he believes "it would ruin us financially." So, at age sixty-two, he will remain in Los Angeles while she traipses off to Costa Rica to find herself and, presumably, the joys of polyamory.

I can hardly hear what he is saying, though I'm connected to a dozen cell towers that incessantly blink from distant hills, like alien scarecrows who stand over us menacingly, reminding us, "We are here, and we have the power to render you mute."

"Hey, Joe Cocker died," he tells me, abruptly changing the subject.

"Yeah, I saw that."

"It's hard to see your heroes die."

My mind makes the necessary leaps to understand why Joe Cocker would be a likely hero to Marcus. Yes, yes, musicians, both of them, although Marcus' music is nothing at all like Joe Cocker's.

And then Marcus says just the kind of thing that explains why I love him, and why we have stayed friends for more than thirty years: "I guess it's time to get new heroes."

It's tough to face the fact that we're growing older, especially for the generation whose mantra was "Don't trust anyone over thirty" and who inspired the phrase, "Sixty is the new forty." My friends and I, spanning in age from the late fifties to the early seventies, have a hard time believing that we will not be "forever young." Many of us still have dreams to fulfill, a long list of adventures to undertake, a world to change. So we are brought up short by the reality of one of our peers, or, worse, one of our heroes, passing over to the other side.

One of my own heroes, though still alive, has recently begun to suffer from a health issue, which has become debilitating enough to affect her ability to think clearly, to read and to write. It was a devastating diagnosis for a writer and poet—words having been her raison d'être, her salvation, her vehicle for transmitting the truth of her life, and for gifting all of us with the brilliance of her insight.

If my generation is delusional about anything, it is the limits of our bodies. In my early forties, a troubling mammogram sent my doctor into alert mode, and he prescribed a biopsy of my right breast. Trying to comprehend his words of alarm, I felt the fist of God strike the middle of my solar plexus. Cancer, I might have cancer, my mind repeated over and over again.

The future, a place we often find ourselves visiting so as to escape the very real and unalterable present, was suddenly off limits. Each breath became at once supremely important and excruciatingly precious. The result of the biopsy was, ultimately, "benign." I was off the hook. But I vowed to never forget that moment and what it felt like to confront death, to meet my mortality face to face.

Years later, in one of our phone conversations, I shared that story with Marcus. He laughed in disbelief. "I've never considered my own death. I plan to live to be a hundred."

And I am convinced he was telling the truth. It had never occurred to him that his body could—in fact, would—take him down. I felt as if I had just disclosed to a four-year-old that there really was no Santa.

The email from my writer friend, in which she described her health crisis, relayed a similar sense of disbelief. It seemed unthinkable to her that her brilliant mind could be stopped, that the thousands of firings of nerves that bring thought into form and communicate information to one's arm, hand, fingers so that a pen can be raised, a computer keyboard tapped, could somehow be eclipsed.

Maybe these understandings—that our lives are finite, that disease, old age, and death are inevitable, that something ultimately will cause our breath to cease—are so difficult to accept for our generation because it came of age in the sixties. This is the generation that stopped a war and participated in the liberation of blacks, women and gays. We rushed the stages of the Beatles, Mick Jagger, Hendrix, and Joplin, made love in the park, and dropped LSD to transform our consciousness and that of the world. Do we hold some wildly ineluctable belief that we will be the generation that beats even death?

Or are we not so different from all the generations before us? Did my mother not cry when her beloved first crush, Frank Sinatra, died, her tears falling for her own lost youth? Did my eighty-five-year-old grandfather not curse the heavens as his heart spasmed and stopped, his body crumpling to the floor, his hands reaching up to his breast pocket where two tickets to Ireland lay in an envelope?

Does each generation "rage against the dying of the light"? Is it part of our humanness to fervently seek life, even as, increasingly, the inevitability of death manifests around us? So Marcus, an aging hippie, looks to date once more; his wife gets on a plane to Costa Rica in search of a rejuvenated love life. I tilt at windmills in the form of cell towers and iPhones, for who knows what reason. Is it because they're too close to the sci-fi fantasies of my youth and I fear they will ultimately be our collective demise? Or is it something far simpler? Perhaps I am not fully able to accept that after I die, life will go on, new technologies will bloom, new heroes will be born, and my one short life will be but a whisper in the trees, a cosmic flash that will exist only as starlight.

We live, we die, as every generation must, no matter how wonderfully wild, woolly and strange a trip it's been. What I wish for myself and for all of us facing that ultimate end: that we live countless more moments filled with what is most significant—and that it may be easy, at the last.

Ominous Visions, or The Twilight Zone

J.D. Rogers

Day One. We were heading into the San Pedro River country in southern Arizona and planned to venture into the Mescal, the Pinaleño, the Galiuo and the Dragoon Mountains. We'd run, crawl or maybe vanish around the Chiricahua National Monument. We wanted to see what the locals in towns like Paradise, Bonita, Pearce, or Gleeson had to offer three outlaws from southeast Utah. All of this would take place over a ten-day road trip of absolute, total debauchery.

My fellow outlaws on this trip were Ricky Lee Costanza, whose punk band, Mucous and the Pussers, were megastars in and around Cisco, Utah, with his hit, "Glow-in-the-Dark Beavers"; and Chris "Madman" Allen, a deranged ex-uranium miner with a knack for chemistry (one should always know a good chemist) and a reincarnated mountain man whose favorite pastime, now that he was enrolled at Utah State University, was watching and cheering for the girls' gymnastics team.

Finding a campsite before dark had always been problematic on our campaigns into the wild backcountry. We knew that around the next bend, over the next mountain, across the next canyon, just a little farther down the road waiting to be discovered was the perfect campsite. We never knew what lay beyond the headlights of "Hank the Tank," Ricky Lee's 1976 white Ford 250 high-boy pickup, sporting Indian blanket seat covers and a gun rack in the back window.

So setting up camp on a dark moonless night was the norm for us. The red-pink painted sky of dawn found us in the middle of clear-cuts, camping under the only five trees left standing. Once we woke up next to a huge crater where nothing lived other than empty broken Tokay wine bottles. (We were only a few feet from a coal strip-mining operation on Black Mesa in the Navajo reservation.)

Day Two. We were wandering down a dusty road on a ridge above the San Pedro River. This area is a vast sea of dehydrated cow pies lying in a moonscape devoid of anything without thorns. God, I love the looks of those cacti: the saguaro with its odd-shaped arms twisting (state of mind) and turning toward the blinding blue sky. Cane cholla, when in bloom, has a beautiful raspberry-purple flower. The Arizona pencil cholla cactus is a good one for body piercing. For the thin-skinned, it's safer to view this countryside from an air-conditioned vehicle.

While making a pit stop, Chris fetched a cold Mickey wide-mouth from the cooler in the pickup bed and spied a nice-looking stone fire ring not too far off this desolate two-track roadway we were on. We drove right over to investigate this as a possible campsite.

This was highly unusual. There was at least an hour of sun left, and yet we were making camp. There was not much shade to be found here, but it was only eighty degrees. The night sky promised to be a fabulous pulsating array of dancing stars.

Ricky Lee got a fire going. When we were down to some good coals, we would be cooking steaks. While sipping his chilled cactus juice and sharing a smoke, Ricky Lee jumped up and asked, "Do you guys hear that?"

Chris said, "Yeah, I do."

I was thankful that someone else heard this. I thought maybe I was slipping into a mental abyss.

A shrill squeal was coming from our burning fire pit.

Using a long-handled shovel, Ricky Lee flipped the burning wood out of the fire pit.

"Oh my god," I cried as he lifted the shovel out of the fire pit.

"Looks like dinner is served," Chris said.

I felt faint, or was that just my state of mind?

What are the odds, I thought. In this backcountry, I'm always on the lookout for rattlesnakes, scorpions, Gila monsters, and tarantulas, but what we found under our fire pit were baby bunnies.

Even though nature provided us with a potential feast, we decided to pass on barbecued bunny and move camp. If we had stayed, I would have had a night of endless nightmares.

We hadn't traveled far when we came to a fork in the road. We took the left fork, which dropped down to the San Pedro River.

"What's that up in the saguaro cactus?" I asked as we started our descent toward the river with the sun low on the colorful western horizon.

Twenty feet up, anchored to the cactus with an arrow, was a javelina head.

As we proceeded down "Javelina Head Road" after leaving "Burnt Bunny Ridge," we wondered what the heck was going on. Were we entering the Twilight Zone? Maybe—we have before.

We found a spot on a bench above the San Pedro River that was shaded with large Fremont cottonwood trees and noticed a lot of recent javelina activity behind our camp—ground rooted up and what looked like old burrows.

As the sun set, we could see thunderclouds building in the distance.

Sitting close to the fire, we hoped the smoke would keep some of the forty species of Arizona mosquitoes at bay. That was all we needed, a little dengue fever, yellow fever, or encephalitis to befall us. How come those bloodsuckers are not on the endangered species list? Even though I know mosquitoes are food for birds and bats, I'm just tired of feeding them. I feared I was becoming anemic.

I was startled out of my dream—where I was battling giant leaches—by the rustling of brush. Something was approaching our camp. While we all breathed quietly, I heard Ricky Lee and Chris each chambering a shell into their firearms. All I had at hand was the stick I'd used earlier to stir the fire. On the far horizon I saw a faint flash of lightning, but heard no thunder.

Chris whispered, "That's not a raccoon family out there. Maybe it's javelinas."

Then out of the night and into our camp walked three snow-white horses. One gave a little snort and pawed the ground. Then I noticed that each horse was watching one of us. One walked up to Ricky Lee and checked him out. Then with a little whinny all ambled on back into the night. Did this really happen? Soon the scent of rain filled the air, and in seconds we were swimming in an Arizona monsoon.

Day Three. The sun's up, the sky is blue, and you can see forever. Hank was covered in mud, but purred down the two-lane blacktop like a well-fed mountain lion.

Wearing only his long johns after his near drowning in the monsoon, Chris was a fashion statement. Between his legs he carried a stainless steel mini-fourteen with a banana clip tightly inserted. The ballcap he was wearing read something like "Die by Thirty."

I knew if the Arizona authorities stopped us now, laxatives would not be needed. Explaining Chris's appearance, let alone our mental state, the eleven o'clock news lead story might have been, "Three radioactive outlaws were dispatched outside of Chiricahua National Monument."

Unfortunately, law enforcement already had Hank's license plate number. Here's why: On the first day of our outing, we started the morning with a Ricky Lee mushroom omelet and were making a refreshment stop while filling Hank with petrol. While in the convenience store not far from the San Carlos Apache Indian Reservation, Chris looked out the store's front window. "We've got trouble," he said. Sure enough, an Arizona trooper was standing behind Hank jotting down our license plate number. Why might he be doing this? Both truck doors were wide open. In the seat sat a bottle of cactus juice and a Mickey's next to a couple of baggies of treats. On the dash was another Mickey's, and the cab had a full gun rack. It looked like natural selection was about to visit us. The officer climbed back into his cruiser with two red cherries on top. We thumbed through the post cards and maps while waiting for him to leave—hoping he would. Ricky Lee said, "When he leaves, we'll go the opposite way and take the first road we come to that heads into the backcountry."

I said, "What if he doesn't leave?"

Silence.

After a short while, which seemed like eternity, the trooper departed.

So far we had been lucky: no further encounters with the authorities. Now we rambled down the two-lane blacktop and turned onto a dirt road that looked like it would take us somewhere, anywhere, a long way from civilization.

We tried to make sense of what we'd been experiencing on this bizarre campaign: police, burnt bunnies, impaled javelina head, three white horses, monsoon rain, and mushroom omelets. Did any of it mean anything? A sign, maybe.

Day Five. We were somewhere in the area known as Cochise's Stronghold, hiking and blazing a trail up into the rocks.

"Ricky Lee, did you lock the truck?" asked Chris.

"No, we only stopped to retrieve some refreshments, and the next thing I know we've been wandering out here for hours."

"You got the keys?" I asked him.

"No, they're in the truck. If I cartwheel over a cliff, you two yahoos can still get your worthless butts out of here."

From above us came a menacing voice. "Hey, white boys, come on up here and see us."

The sun was shining into our eyes, but I could still make out two armed Indians. One of the rifles looked to be a

30-30, but who could tell for sure as we were a ways below them.

As we circled back toward the truck, the voices became more ominous.

"Don't go away, white boys," said one.

"Come up and see us," said the other.

Back at the truck, Chris declared, "We will be armed at all times." Great, all I had was a small Swiss army knife.

With his binoculars Ricky Lee scanned the hillside we had retreated from, but couldn't see any sign of the two armed Indians.

"You know," Ricky Lee said, "We've seen Indians in the distance about every day so far. Always in the distance, and they appear to be watching us."

Was he getting paranoid or succumbing to a mental meltdown due to his years of abusive living? No, Chris and I had also witnessed the watchers.

Had we been stepping in and out of another dimension? I've always been quite certain that Ricky Lee and Chris are from another dimension. Had we been on some sort of vision quest and not known it? Hmm, maybe.

As Chris lit a smoke, he inquired, "You pantywaists want a Mickey's?"

Day Seven. "Where's my bunny bread?" Ricky Lee cried.

"I see a few gnawed-on pieces down in the wash," Chris said.

The night before, we stumbled onto this nice campsite. This was the first developed campsite we'd found on this outing. We had two nice picnic tables under magnificent

Fremont cottonwood trees, a metal fire ring, and level ground overlooking a dry wash.

Immediately, Chris saw an enormous white feral cat watching us from the other side of the wash. The kitty eyed us from different places from across the wash until it was too dark for us to see it.

After we melted into our sleeping bags for the night, our camp was covertly raided. Come daylight, we had "The Case of the Missing Bunny Bread."

What is bunny bread? Any white bread that can be rolled into a tight ball and floated in chocolate milk without absorbing any liquid. Ricky Lee loves his chocolate floaters to this day.

Chris's and my one hundred percent whole wheat bread was still intact in our food box as were our Twinkies, cookies, potato chips, and baggies of other much-needed survival edibles.

"Check out these tracks, Ricky Lee. These belong to a thieving house cat," Chris said with a chuckled.

While our camp had been under siege, the only casualty had been the white bunny bread, stolen by the white cat that was yet again spying on us from across the sandy wash.

The few slices of bunny bread that were left in the shredded bag had curled and stiffened in the dry Arizona air. The ants, however, still showed interest in the mummified remains.

Was this another sign? Were the gods speaking to us, or were we lost in some alien-induced dream world?

After Ricky Lee recovered from his traumatic loss, he was able to make his magical mushroom omelets before we broke camp.

Day Nine. I still hadn't seen the beautiful red summer tanager, the varied bunting, or the western tanager, or any of the other one hundred species of birds that live in this area. However, we had seen turkey vultures circling overhead every day.

Tombstone, founded in 1879, was the last of the wide-open frontier boomtowns. Now it caters to the pampered western Disneyland-type crowds. I've had a few wild adventures among Tombstone's fake gunfights, fake cowboys, and wooden headstones painted, "George Johnson, Hanged by Mistake."

Today is Chris's birthday, and we planned to celebrate at a bar called Johnny Ringo's, but it had burned to the ground. While standing on its remains, we told Ricky Lee what a fabulous dump it had once been. We had placed bets on cockroaches racing as they scurried down the bar. We always kept our feet moving so our shoes wouldn't stick in the unknown biohazardous substance oozing across the floor.

What I really loved about Ringo's was the glass-fronted enclosure occupied by an 1800s buggy with a skeleton seated on it. The skeleton wore an old cavalry uniform with a couple of arrows protruding from it. The scene was complete with sand, cactus, and a couple of large, live rattlesnakes.

The only downside to this dark, dank establishment was when answering nature's call, you had to hold your breath upon entering the latrine, which hadn't been cleaned since 1899. Even with a broken window, you knew how World War I soldiers experienced being gassed. Your eyes always teared up and your lungs burned before you could exit.

Tombstone's Big Nose Kate Saloon is where we put down roots for the evening. We met a busload of tourists on a sightseeing tour. When we told them we were celebrating Chris's birthday, they bought us drinks.

One of the ladies asked Chris what he did for a living.

"I'm a doctor," he said.

"Oh, where did you go to school?"

"Johns Hopkins."

"That's where my granddaughter is going!"

"Imagine that," said Chris.

"What sort of doctor are you?"

"Gynecologist."

Ricky Lee told the group that he was the bodyguard for the unknown rock star—that would be me, and they bought us more drinks.

While some of the women were asking Chris questions about their medical conditions, Ricky Lee was explaining gun safety to some of the folks from Cleveland, Ohio, the Cool Whip consumption capital of the country.

Me? I had met a local maiden who said she was going on a vision quest into the desert. Did I want to join her?

Hacking Stream Restoration:
The Exiled Hydro Engineer

Kirsten K. Shockey

If I ever go to jail, it will be for aiding and abetting a large rodent.

My family and I are fortunate, in a semiarid climate, to be stewards of a property with three ponds, a year-round spring, and a creek that delivers high mountain water to the Applegate River, which pours into the Rogue River and finally empties into the Pacific Ocean. We are post-modern homesteaders on hardscrabble steep land. I have heard this area called "poverty with a view." Small farms and ranches dot the area around the creek, but our principal neighbors are the remote forested ridges and their wild inhabitants. We have bears and cougars. Deer and wild turkeys eat my garden and fruit trees. An abundance of squirrels, less common western pond turtles, rare Pacific fishers, salamanders, steelhead, and salmon live in and around the waterways that cross our farm. Bald eagles and golden eagles, red-tailed hawks, and the occasional blue heron fly overhead. We hope there are spotted owls. We have dominion of forty acres in the roughly 23,000 acres of slopes, forested or meadowed, that make up our valley. These slopes are veined with steep tributaries that swell and eventually feed the creek that winds across our property at the valley floor. Yet this basin, as far as I know, does not accommodate a single North American beaver (*Castor canadensis*).

We are also well into a drought cycle. Our spring is a trickle, and the last two years the creek has been dry by June. Coho and chinook are in peril.

Contemplating a life of crime began innocently enough. Every year in the late part of the winter our favorite tree climber comes to prune seven pioneer-planted apple trees. Let's call him Erich. Our dignified trees speak to him. He feels their strength and health and often tells me of their moods. Four years ago, while Erich sat perched on a limb, he looked out across the creek and casually mentioned beavers. "Have you ever thought about beavers living on your part of the creek?" he asked.

"I would love to see beavers living here," I said without hesitation.

"Great," he said, "I know somebody who occasionally needs to find a home for beavers. He's on the local watershed council; he gets calls from distraught homeowners when beavers move onto their property. He likes to have relocation sites lined up owned by beaver friendly folks. It's an underground operation." Erich paused and looked at me. "You know you will lose some trees, right?"

"I know; it's okay," I said, glancing at the alders, cedars, and maples I knew intimately, having watched them daily through seasons and storms.

"All right, I will let him know."

His words ignited something in me. I learned everything I could about beavers. My mantra became, "Build it, and they will come." Coerced into helping, my children and I planted many willow twigs along the creek, all the while waiting for the phone to ring, telling me a delivery would be made that night. The phone never rang.

It is nothing short of ironic that in the Beaver State I can legally kill a beaver on my land, but I cannot legally move a beaver to or from my land. Only a licensed trapper can move a beaver. Unfortunately, no one can release a live beaver on public land or on private land (with one exception). On private land, these strictly vegetarian rodents are classified as predatory animals. I cannot allow an unwanted beaver family that has been legally live-trapped to be moved here. The exception is for me (the landowner) to get signed permission from each of my neighbors within six miles, upstream and down, of our farm—only a few hundred awkward conversations. Our diverse neighbors are a blend of organic farmers, retirees—transplants from many walks of life—and a few remaining locals, whose families homesteaded here a century ago. The very wealthy live alongside the very poor.

I do know from casual conversations that most of our neighbors would agree that beavers are fine—somewhere else. Like prisons or landfills, they provide a needed function as long as they're "not in my backyard." Long-held beliefs that beavers steal water, eat all the fish, and are destructive run deep in the collective psyche. I realize, even with sound scientific evidence to the contrary, that traipsing from door to door advocating for the beaver would not change most people's minds. I would rather sign up for an unnecessary root canal.

"Let them live in the forest lands" is a common sentiment. However, our high mountain landscape is ancient and rugged, and the streams are rocky. Water tumbling down steep slopes makes it too difficult for these rodents to build and maintain a dam. Even in 1828 trappers did not find beavers in these mountains. The ideal beaver habitat is along low-gradient valley waterways where people live, own land, and make their livelihoods. Conflict arises as humans and beavers want to live along the same watercourses. The North

American Beaver is just another player in the race for water rights.

Surprisingly, even armchair environmentalists and advocates of creeks as wildlife corridors do not want beavers to reclaim their homes on the creeks. Recently an article in a local newspaper reported that beavers had thwarted students' restoration efforts along an "embattled stream." Indeed, Bear Creek suffers, as it is situated alongside the west coast's major transportation corridor, Interstate 5. When I read that beavers had returned, I thought: Awesome! Let the real restoration begin. I believe that the students' project leader agrees, yet he still insists the beavers be moved "where they could use their engineering skills and tree-poaching prowess to help create fish habitat." Students are taught that the beaver is ruining their hard work until "this vandal gets its eviction notice." What kind of message is this? As scientists throughout the world are starting to agree that repatriating streams with beaver may be the only way to combat the mounting water crisis, the local district wildlife biologist supports the same old disconnected thinking: "Beavers are a nuisance problem and cause grief to people wherever they go." What?

When beavers set up a home, debris and sediment back up behind their dam. Instantly, hydrology of the stream changes, as the water now collects in pools and backwaters, creating a varied habitat for the return of other species missing in the ecosystem—turtles, otters, muskrats, waterfowl, fish, and salamanders. Allowing beavers to reclaim their place on our watercourses is not only about the beavers. It is about us, the humans, allowing these natural engineers to help us to mend, maintain, and preserve the natural resources for which we have assumed responsibility through our history of alterations.

Imagine beads on a string, bobbles of different shapes and sizes—oblong and round, teardrops and bubbles. These strings of beaver dams wound like rickrack through bottomlands and across plains, moving through the landscape, one beaver dam after another causing the fresh water to move unhurried to the ocean. Before French and English trappers came to these streams to satiate the mania for felted beaver-fur hats that swept early nineteenth century Europe and the burgeoning United States, these still-water pools recharged the groundwater and widened the greenbelts throughout what is now the United States and Canada. Beaver ponds provided habitat for ninety percent of all wildlife at some stage in their development and are increasingly important today for endangered and threatened species of amphibians, fish, mammals, and fowl that struggle for fading habitat. The beaver's work sequesters surface water and helps to recharge our groundwater.

We are in a drought cycle. Our creeks are drying earlier and earlier in the spring, and there is not enough water for coho and chinook to spawn successfully in the fall. When they spawn, their fry swim in increasingly smaller pools until they gasp on hot, dry rocks. We need the help of the beavers.

The health and fertility of the larger landscape and the resilience of the upland forest ecosystems depend on the matrix created by the giant vegetarian rodent. In the Northwest, the fertility of the forests was directly correlated to the streams that ran so thick with salmon that the bears and other animals could pluck them from the water. The carcasses were dropped for centuries throughout the uplands, the marine nitrogen providing nourishment to the soil and vegetation.

The winter following that day under the apple tree, I met my tribe. I attended the first State of the Beaver Conference where "beaver believers" from across the United States and Canada gathered in Canyonville, Oregon, just an hour and a half from my home. A few attendees had come from as far as Scotland and Norway. Passion ran high. On the afternoon of the first day, following a morning of scientific PowerPoint presentations, Sherrie Tippie took the podium to tell us her story. Years ago she refused to let the city of Denver bully a beaver family. A hairdresser by trade and with no experience in conservation work, she moved the beavers herself and since has made advocating for and moving beavers her life's work. Sherrie is a key player in the movement of people who believe beavers play a role in mitigating climate change.

At the beaver conference I learned words like sinuosity, geomorphology, and turbidity. I learned that the waterways we know today are often incised with steep, straight-sided banks, that the grass stops at this bank and the buffers of riparian trees are thin and park-like. The problem is that this path-of-least-resistance efficiency sends fresh water rushing to the ocean, taking the banks along with it. Sedimentation of the streams causes problems for aquatic life, and the flush of earthy minerals into the sea contributes to the acidification of the ocean.

A few years ago I stood in a drought-parched streambed talking with a geologist who engineers log structures that are part of our local watershed restoration projects. I'll call him Max. I met Max at the State of the Beaver Conference. Max designed twenty-six structures for 2.1 contiguous miles of our creek. The first stream mile holds very few bends. In 1964, after a bank-breaching deluge, a local bulldozer operator is said to have driven down the middle of the creek pushing the bed into berms to keep the surges in the straight and narrow. Max's work is designed to create curves and bends to turn the streambed from a ditch-like passage to the mountain stream that it is. For a year, he repeatedly walked the channel, creating diagrams to show where and how each structure worked with the others to change the hydrology and give it complexity.

Last spring, Max combed Bureau of Land Management forests for snags (dead standing trees) with intact root wads. The wads were marked, dragged from the forest, hauled to a staging area, crane-loaded onto trucks, and towed to the creek. Now, under Max's careful eye, heavy machinery digs, tugs, and heaves, knitting these root balls into the bank where they will stay for many years. Each of Max's constructions is a weaving of three or more logs that are dug into the channels to mimic a wild creek bed. These structures will cause the water to carve out pools to give the fish a safe place to grow and help cool the water in the dry months and slow it down in the rainy season. Sounds a lot like an expensive beaver dam.

Max replicates the missing beaver dams. He also knows that beavers plan and build their dams for free. Max has spent over a decade advocating for these wild engineers, as well as covertly relocating them along creeks that need their help.

We can responsibly relocate beavers using a Hancock live trap, a clamshell, chain-linked affair that is affixed overnight to the banks of a waterway. Relocation can take upwards of seventy hours. Beavers have strong family units that should be kept together. Part of the commitment requires going back to the site daily to account for every member of the family. Ideally relocators would hold the beavers until they could release them as a family, but state agency rules dictate immediate release. The best time to relocate families is when the kits are old enough to move safely and have the skills to find their parents even after a few days of separation.

Max no longer moves beavers and has given up trying to change people's minds. "It may be that beavers and people just are incompatible," he told me that day. I felt a small disheartening shadow move across my desire to see beavers return.

I nodded and looked down to our pasture, separated from the creek by a neat, shallow line of alders. I wanted to feel optimistic, but I wasn't sure what to say. "Isn't it just that it is too random? A beaver in the neighborhood is like having an unpredictable whimsical landscaper, felling some trees and building large water features, redesigning the landscape without our approval."

I was thinking about a conversation I'd had with a friend, a highly educated, environmentally motivated type. She was incensed that a beaver moved into their pond and Fish and Wildlife refused to move it because the season was wrong. I told her to call me before she shot it. She didn't call, either.

Maybe it is just too hard to see the initial change as anything more than a damaging wound on the land, but don't we create such wounds all the time with our machinery? Earthmoving bulldozers or excavators, dump trucks that haul away or bring anew, even plows and rototillers, or saws and axes—all produce scars. We should try to see past the change and forward to the resulting beauty that develops with all its intricacies, over time. After all, beavers are second to us in their ability to change a landscape. A landscape altered by beavers creates some of the most picturesque and productive freshwater wetlands on earth, teeming with biodiversity that rivals that of tropical rainforests.

I still have hope that we can reconnect with beavers and let the wildness of their families into our neighborhoods and our lives. Meanwhile, I will continue to build an inviting beaver habitat in hope that they will come and reclaim what is theirs. I protect my favorite trees with a bit of fence around their bases. I continue to plant willow branches. And if I go to jail for moving a beaver, it will definitely be a premeditated crime.

Cycles
Thalia Truesdell

Rumbling, rolling, and wearing, the boulders traveled, heaved, settled, and rolled again. Rocks cracked and shattered in the confusion, grinding into sand, depositing themselves in pockets where the river swirled against its banks. Tumultuous floods, gentle hoar frosts, shale landslides, and the activity of beavers over eons moved, dammed, hurled, jammed, and settled the boulders, sand, and the gold, as the river cut new channels or lazily meandered through emerald pools, hosts to generations of industrious salmon. Ah, the gold.

Then came then the miners, driven by greed. Reaching into the depths of the river, wrenching, removing, and exploding boulders in their search for the elusive gold that had settled deep into the bedrock crevices, the miners began to alter what Mother Earth had spent thousands of years creating. Rock by rock, carried by hand, tossed by shovel, hoisted by pulleys, or hauled by mules, miners created portable mountains next to the river. Some of these mountains of rock, called tailings piles, were taller than buildings. They lined the river for miles.

Lizards scurried over the new formations, rattlesnakes sunned themselves on the warm rocks in the spring sunshine, and children played King of the Mountain, helping the rocks settle a little more comfortably together. An occasional squirrel skittered by, cheeks fat with acorns, en route to an oak tree where its winter stash lay hidden.

Lichen eventually took hold on the stones, slowly spreading, gradually changing the color of the piles from grays to greens. Acorns took root, and young trees emerged and struggled in the desolate rock piles. Fir needles, oak leaves, and dust settled deep into the crevices, creating a welcome environment for other seeds, and life began to flourish between the rocks.

As the trees grew and began to shade the mountains of rubble, moss emerged slowly at first, cautiously shrouded in the shady, moist cracks and offering solace to tiny animals, who helped contribute to the viability of the man-made mountains. Generations later, that moss had become a velvet, verdant carpet, and many of the tailings piles had become inviting features of the landscape, tucked in shady glens under towering firs and wide, spreading oaks.

Thunderheads skimmed over the ridgetops, uniting, billowing, and darkening. All eyes turned upwards, analyzing the clouds, praying for rain to accompany the inevitable thunderstorm and cursing the drought that left the forest so frighteningly vulnerable.

The forest service lookout, in his perch high on Blue Ridge, was the first to see a lightning strike, then another, and another. Crews were assembled and dispatched to the areas struck by lightning, but the dry vegetation tenaciously grabbed hold of the sparks and turned them into raging forest fires. Locals formed themselves into their own fire crew, calling themselves the Salmon River Hillbillies and offering what protection they could to the threatened homes and structures. Statewide resources were stretched thin, and the sparsely populated Salmon River was the lowest on the priority lists. As the fires intensified, residents were ordered to evacuate, but they held their ground, added more water lines, which later melted, and did all they could to save their homes.

Over the next few weeks the fury of the fire was unleashed on the Salmon River drainage. Fingers of angry flame shot up draws, defying all efforts to stop them. Ancient fir trees, several feet in diameter, exploded like Roman candles, shooting swirls of burning needles and deadly flames high into the smoky skies, the embers catching the wind and lighting fires on nearby ridges.

Some of the fires raced through areas of the forest, burning only the lower branches of the trees and all the ground cover, yet sparing some canopy, which may live, and if so, will help shield the ground and aid in regrowth. Some of the burns are thickly mulched with fir and pine needles that fell off the burned trees after the fires had passed, leaving in their wake hundreds of acres of standing toothpicks, seemingly devoid of life. Many of the fires burned hot and furious enough to destroy everything in their paths, resulting in charred trunks, some left standing amid a deep bed of blackened limbs, choking ash, and vanished needles. And then it was gone, this destructive monster that devoured the landscape, the wildlife, and the heart of the mountains, the rain-soaked charcoal leaving a putrid stink as a reminder of its fury. The rich, mossy fairy lands, the twentieth century's painstakingly slow creations, have returned to naked tailings piles. These miniature ecosystems, once teeming with life, the deep moss hiding the salient evidence of a century's intense mining activity, have been reduced to piles of rocks.

But here, at the base of a huge live oak, its charred silhouette stately in the foreground of the devastated mountain behind it, sprouts a slender two-inch stem with six tender green leaves, and a lizard suns itself on a blackened stone in the autumn sunshine.

~ FICTION ~

Tune in, Drop out

Dolores Durando

In the paper the place was advertised as a charming old farmhouse with a red barn, complete with apple trees, chickens, and even a pond, just ten miles from the sleepy little town of Santa Rosa.

To this I brought six retarded foster children and my young son, who had returned from San Francisco and brought his problems with him.

I looked out the window to see the old handyman struggling with a roll of wire.

"Mr. Hogan," I called, "you will need to pull that wire higher and tighter."

I walked out, picked up his hammer, and with a few quick blows drove in the staples.

"See. Like that."

I could hear the phone's insistent ringing as I drove in another staple and finally handed the hammer to the old man and ran to the house.

As I lifted the receiver I heard the frantic voice of a girl. "Get Stevie out of there—now! J.D. is coming to kill him."

Stevie had lifted the phone on the extension and said dully, "It's okay, Francie. I owe him some money. I'll just pay him. Don't worry, it's okay."

"No, Stevie, no," she sobbed, but he had already hung up and stumbled back to bed.

I hovered anxiously in the doorway.

"Stevie, what's happening? Who is J.D.? Why do you owe him money?"

"It's okay, Mom," he mumbled. "I'll take care of it."

I agonized. Where is he getting these drugs? Where is he getting the money to buy them?

It was the heyday of the flower children—the Summer of Love. If it feels good, do it. Tune in, drop out. The time of Timothy Leary.

Drugs were as foreign to me as opium dens in China. Uppers, downers, LSD, Mary Jane—what did it all mean? Nothing to me, but now this hideous habit was in my home slowly devouring the life of my beloved son.

Wearily I returned to the fence-building. My mind raced over the insanity that had haunted me for the past two years.

My family said, "You must have done something horrible to him to have driven him to drugs."

The doctor said, "Thorazine is the answer."

The police said, "We have no drug problem in our town."

The church said, "We'll pray for you, sister."

Somewhere in the back of my mind I remembered the words, "Faith without works is dead."

As if in a never-ending nightmare, I watched helplessly as my firstborn son sank deeper and deeper into the quicksand that I feared would take his sanity first and then his life.

"Hey, missus, looks like you got company," the handyman said, and I looked up to see an old car painted with psychedelic colors and festooned with peace signs winding down the long driveway. It came to a stop and a tall, strange-looking man stepped out. He wore a long black old-fashioned frock coat, and his hair hung heavy and black over his shoulders.

As I looked into those cold black eyes, fear swept over me like an ocean wave.

"What do you want?" I asked.

"I've come for Stevie."

"He's not here. If he owes you money, I'll pay you." My voice seemed to choke in my throat.

"Oh, yes, he's here and I want him. I'm going to teach him a lesson he'll remember—if he makes it through the course."

"Please," I begged him. "Let me pay you."

"You ain't got enough money, lady."

"Get off my property. I'll call the police. I'll set this dog on you."

"Do that, and I promise you a dead dog. By the time the police get here, I'll be gone. What would they charge me with —trespassing? You're kinda fun to talk with, lady. I'll be back."

It was later, and dark, when the dog barked at the strangely colored car that parked almost on the patio at the back of the house, the headlights blazing through the big picture windows.

The man stepped out and walked to the patio.

"Ooooh, Stevie...I see you..." came his cruel, singsong voice.

"Stevie, please don't go out there, Stevie. No!"

"Don't worry, Mom. Stay here—I'll take care of this."

I followed.

As Stevie approached, the man stepped to meet him, grabbed him by the back of the neck, dragged him to the car and smashed his head against the side. Not once, but time and again. Stevie went limp.

Screaming, I ran up the man's back like a cat, clawing, digging at his face. Then I crouched next to my son.

"You'll have to take me, too," I yelled as I wrapped my arms around Stevie.

The man tried to pull me away, but no power on earth could part me from my son.

Finally he had us in the car—I was still screaming, kicking, struggling.

"Oh, to hell with it." He planted his foot in my back and pushed us out on the ground.

"Don't get comfortable. I'll be back, you hellcat. You'll get yours."

I called the police at two AM and sobbed out the entire story, my son's involvement with drugs no longer of primary importance.

How to survive this horror?

The young policeman was sympathetic, but explained that until this person had actually done something, they had nothing to charge him with and could not help.

In desperation, I said, "I'll have to kill him."

"Do that," the policeman advised. "Drag him over the threshold and let him bleed on the floor. Sorry, missus."

The old car chugged up the driveway three more nights. Always the same dialogue, always the same laughter as I pleaded. He was enjoying himself as he told me about his plans for Stevie.

Three sleepless nights of terror hung over me like a shroud. Days filled with endless work as I cared for six retarded children. Nights I lay stiff with fear, anticipating the sound of that car coming down the driveway. It all finally took its toll and brought the sure realization that there was no one to turn to. My son's life depended solely on me.

I walked across the pasture to my neighbor and asked if I could borrow his shotgun. I told him that my livestock were being harassed by a pack of dogs.

He loaded the double-barreled gun and cautioned, "Now, missus, be careful. I know you have those children there, and this is a very dangerous weapon. It's deadly at close range, but if you should miss, it will probably scare those dogs to death."

As I carried it home, I felt a crushing weight being lifted from my shoulders.

I knew what I had to do and never gave the consequences a moment's thought. There was no other way, and, at last, I had peace of mind.

The gun seemed light as a feather as I lifted it to a high shelf in the back porch.

I was relieved that night, almost happy, when I heard the car. I glanced at the clock. One fifteen AM.

I took the gun down and set it just inside the back door that opened to the patio as a thought passed through my mind: The noise will scare the kids to death, and I'll be up all night.

He parked. The headlights that shined behind him seemed to make a ten-foot shadow.

"Good evening, lady. Are you ready for this?" came the same cruel, mocking voice that had earlier assured me, "You've given me so much trouble—your turn is next, bitch."

He walked confidently across the patio. Each night he had come closer, and now there was twenty feet between our life and his death.

I spoke slowly and clearly.

"This is the last time you are going to come here."

He laughed and said easily, "You're right. Tonight is the night. I've wasted enough time. You are going to bring him out, or I am coming in—and then it's your turn."

I reached behind me and lifted the gun. As I hugged it into my shoulder, it seemed weightless. I said quietly, almost in a whisper, my eyes never leaving his, "I am going to kill you."

In the silence that seemed to last forever, I could hear the noisy crickets, the croaking of the frogs in the pond, and a sharp intake of breath—the sound of his suddenly harsh breathing.

I held the gun steady with an overpowering sense of relief —now it would be over. We could live again, and I would find help somewhere, somehow for the son that was my life.

From miles away I heard this little boy's voice. How odd, I thought. That almost sounds like Stevie when he was in the first grade.

Time stood still.

"For god's sake, lady, please…please! My mother would die if you killed me."

As I continued to hold the gun steady, somewhere in my mind I could visualize this man's mother, who loved her son as unconditionally as I loved mine. Then I imagined my words to her: "Your son is dead, that mine might live."

"Please, lady. In the name of God! I am her only son."

He trembled so, I thought he'd fall.

A twitch of my finger and he'll be dead.

But my mind persisted: Your son isn't innocent. How do you know he hasn't been responsible for some other mother's heartbreak and prayers?

Then this mother, unknown to me, who had given this man life, now gave it to him, again.

Suddenly the gun weighed more than I could hold. I lowered it to the floor.

I spoke so quietly, almost doubting I was speaking at all.

"Go. Go then and never come back."

"I never will," he answered.

As the taillights disappeared into the darkness, I walked into Stevie's room and pulled up the covers. Then I sank on my own bed, said my prayers, and went to sleep.

La Bella Rosa

Laurie Easter

The doctor, the nurses, the receptionist—they all said it was to be a routine checkup. Lucia said there was nothing to worry about. She would be fine. She could get herself to the hospital and back again, no problem. She would meet me for dinner at La Bella Rosa. We would eat lasagna and drink cabernet and listen to *The Marriage of Figaro*, and then we'd eat zabaglione with amaretti and drink cognac. Afterwards, we would walk the streets in the fog. It would be dark and damp. The streets would be peaceful and lonely and quiet.

"Would you like to dance, *signor*?" she would ask.

"*Si*, my sweet *bella rosa*," I'd say.

And I'd twirl her under my arm. She'd laugh, and I would bow, my stiff right leg cumbersome. We would go to the motel on the corner, the one with the flashing red light: vacancy, vacancy, vacancy. We'd ask for the room, the one on the corner overlooking the streets. They would have saved it for us.

That morning Lucia left me with my coffee and roll at the café. I watched her hips curve down the street atop her slender legs. The sun was bright, and there were no clouds in the sky. It was very warm for February. The downtown bustle reached maximum around nine AM: the baker delivered his rounds of bread and rolls to the restaurants, the produce man filled his stand along the sidewalk, the butcher cut shanks of beef. It must be Tuesday, for the line went out the butcher's door and half a block down the street, filled with all sorts: creased, old women; mothers with grimy-handed children;

men who looked half-starved. They all wanted meat. It was so hard to come by.

I did my usual share of meeting with the others on leave from the front lines. We would drink and smoke and play cards. Sometimes we'd read magazine articles to each other. We stayed away from the post. Not one of us wanted to know what was going on. We just wanted to enjoy our time away, pretend the war didn't exist. We would start at the café and then move to the bar. Eventually, we'd each go separate ways. Mine was always to meet Lucia. By that time, she would be done with work and ready to eat and drink and dance. But that day I didn't make it to *La Bella Rosa*.

Just before eleven AM, there was a siege on the city. Tanks thundered down the avenues, stopping for no one. I watched, from inside Frank's bar, a mother screaming. Her little boy couldn't run fast enough and disappeared underneath the rolling metal feet. Rico went to stop her from running underneath the machine herself. He pulled her inside the bar and held her, sobbing and shuddering. Then the explosions started—mostly grenades thrown from the tanks. But a few planes passed overhead, dropping missiles on the town, in the eastern quarter, across the canal, over near the hospital. I thought of Lucia. She would have been to the hospital and back by now. She would be at work. There, she would be safe. It was a strong building. She had a hard desk to hide under.

It didn't last long, an hour, maybe. But everyone was too frightened to go out. So we stayed put. Drinks were on the house that afternoon. Frank kept refilling the empty glasses.

"*Grazie*," we said over and over.

"*Pensare nulla di esso*," he said, with a wave of his hand. Think nothing of it.

By six thirty PM darkness came, and the town was calm enough for us to go out. Rico escorted home the woman who had lost her son. She leaned heavily on him. He practically had to drag her, for her legs would not work properly. Frank invited us to stay, but I said, "*Arrivederci*," and started towards *La Bella Rosa*.

The downtown was in pieces. The produce stand was a wreck: oranges scattered and squished everywhere, their pulp splattered on walls, over the sidewalk, in the street. The butcher's window was gone. The smell of burnt raw meat hung in the air. Flies buzzed in and out through the broken glass. Inside, the butcher swept the same spot over and over. A block away, under one of the few remaining street lamps, I saw a woman's figure approach. My insides rushed at the sight of her, then faltered. It was not her. It was not my Lucia. I recognized her, though. Allessandra was her name, Lucia's friend and coworker.

"*Buona sera*, Allessandra!" I called out to her.

"Richard! You must come. Come right away," she called back.

"What is it, Allessandra? Are you hurt?"

"It is Lucia. She never made it to work today! She called from the hospital after her appointment. She said she was leaving and would be there soon. But then the tanks, and the bombs...."

I took Allessandra's arm, and together we walked towards the hospital. "She's probably been hiding. I'm sure she's all right. We'll find her," I said. But I felt sick. *My Lucia. My sweet bella rosa.*

We walked the half hour to the hospital. The bridges had been taken out by the missiles, so the only way to cross the canal was in a little rowboat that a man sat in waiting for patrons. "*Buona sera!*" he called to us. "*Cinque lire*, and I'll take you across." What choice did we have but to pay?

Chaos—that was the hospital. Many injured had been brought there and now lay moaning and bleeding on gurneys. Others sat in chairs, holding bandages to their wounds.

"*Scusi*, we are looking for someone," I said to the nurse behind the counter. "A woman, Lucia Santorelli."

She told us to sit and wait, everyone was looking for somebody.

"*Scusi*, we need to find her. *Per favore*, can you check? She had an appointment here this morning, just before the bombs."

The nurse found Lucia's name on the roster. "Yes," she told us. "She was here, signed out at 10:45. If she came back in, I wouldn't know it. Too many to keep track of, and nobody has papers. But you could check the basement."

"The basement?" we said.

"*Si*. That's where they take the dead."

In the basement, we walked down the dark and narrow corridor toward the swinging double doors. I held onto Allessandra so she would not collapse. The stench of formaldehyde and blood left a sour taste, and the cold air made me sweat. "She is not here," I said. "We will only check to rule out the possibility." Allessandra nodded. "She is probably waiting for me at *La Bella Rosa*. She must be worried so, with my absence."

A big man in a dirty white coat came through the double doors and asked if we were there to identify. Yes, I said, we were there to identify, but we would be wasting his time. The woman we were looking for wouldn't be in such a hard, sterile room. She was probably waiting for me at our favorite restaurant, and she would be very distraught over my tardiness.

"A woman you say? What are her identifying features? Say, her clothes? Her hair?" the man in the dirty coat asked.

"Black hair, shoulder length, wavy. She was wearing a plaid skirt and wool cardigan sweater. I'm sure you have not seen her."

The man in the coat said nothing. He walked over to one of the many sheet-covered gurneys and read the attached tag. Then he pulled back the sheet.

There she was. *My Lucia.*

"Is this her?" he asked.

Allessandra began to cry.

"Yes," I said. "That is her."

"What is her name?" the man asked.

"Rosa," I said. "*Bella Rosa.*"

The Old Storyteller
Morgan Jordan

Danville, Arkansas
1952

In winter Grandpa placed a board over the screen in Donnie Marie's bedroom window to keep her warm. In summer the board came down. Fireflies and stars would twinkle her away into dreams. She had come to their old farmhouse to stay for a while because her mama was sick. The house was an asbestos covered, tar papered, ancient place with a barn Grandpa had built with his sons—one of them her daddy—years before she was born. They had screened in the porch at the back of the house because the mosquitos were so bad Grandpa said they could carry away a whole hog. Of course she'd never seen this happen and figured Grandpa liked to say things to make you see pictures in your mind. When she questioned him with a dimple and a smile, he'd just say, "Would I lie?"

The sun is at the back of the house visiting the soft round hills. Grandma and Donnie are done with the supper dishes. "Go on now. Grandpa's on the front porch. I'll be along directly."

Donnie Marie steps out into the fading day and catches sight of the old tree, begging to be climbed.

"Hold on there," calls Grandpa, halting her descent into the heady sweet spice of the cool green yard. "It's not a good time to go out in the grass. Wait'll the snakes get settled."

"Snakes?" Quickly backing up the steps, Donnie Marie drops down on the floor of the porch beside the long thin man.

Carefully trimming his nails with his pen knife and without looking up, Grandpa says, "Why don't you go get yourself a chair?"

"No need," says Grandma, pushing open the screen. She sets a stool down. "Here ya go. Climb up, and mind you don't lean back on the legs."

Donnie Marie obeys and turns to Grandpa. "Are there really snakes in the yard?"

The soft brown eyes shift their gaze upon her, and Grandpa asks, "Would I lie?"

Donnie Marie begins to contemplate the answer when the soft lilt of Grandpa's voice begins again. "Now, there's all kinds of snakes, you know. Some are to be feared, and some are our friends."

Her mouth falls open, pure disbelief in her blue-green eyes.

"You don't believe me," the old man says. He takes a stone from his pocket, spits on it, and begins sharpening his knife. "Well, let me see. It was...well, I reckon it was about this time o' the year when Charlie and his wife Bessie was sittin' on the porch. 'Bout like we're a-doin' right now. Now, Charlie, he fixed his eyes on their long dirt driveway and said nothin', just kept a starin'. Pretty soon Bessie noticed and said, 'Charlie, what you lookin' at?'" Donnie Marie smiles when Grandpa crackles his voice like Bessie Porter.

"Charlie motioned her to be quiet," Grandpa continues, stretching his long finger out toward the dirt path leading to the farmhouse. "Then he pointed. Bessie looked. Why, there in the driveway, sliding on up towards them through the dust, was a big ol' king snake."

Donnie Marie sits up straight on the seat and follows Grandpa's finger with her eyes.

The gentle voice slips through the air. "That snake must have been about six feet long an' all dusty from his a-crawlin' through the dirt. He was 'bout as thick around as my leg." Grandpa slaps his thigh and then begins to move his arm from side to side. "He just kept on a-slidin' up towards them weavin' this-a-way and that-a-way.

"'Charlie, you best go get your gun. That snake is a-comin' this way and it don't look like he's gonna stop,' Bessie said."

Grandpa looks at Donnie Marie and smiles. Leaning over he squints down their drive as if he was watching a snake come up towards their house. "Charlie said, 'Hold on Bess. Let's just see what he's up to.'"

The storyteller winks at Donnie Marie and says, "Well now, Bessie, she was not likin' this one bit. But she waited with Charlie and watched that snake a-comin' closer and closer, and then it turned. And what do you know but that ole' boy began slitherin' right on up the steps a' their front porch."

Donnie Marie can't help it. She darts her eyes toward the steps and squinches herself closer to Grandpa, expecting the head of that giant king snake to appear, weaving and making its way onto *their* porch.

"Bessie was really beginning to worry now," says Grandpa, wrapping his arm around Donnie Marie's shoulders. "She said, 'Charlie you best get your gun. He's a-comin' up here on the porch!' But Charlie just said, 'Hesh up, woman. I want to see what he's up to.'"

A sweet honeysuckle breeze blows across the yard, stirring and swooshing through the leaves on the oak tree. Off somewhere across the road the long, high-pitched whistle of a warbler reaches the three souls sitting on the porch in the Arkansas sunset. Grandma is quiet, sitting next to Grandpa on the bench, reading her bible and smiling. She takes off her glasses and wipes her eyes. Donnie Marie sees the tears. Grandma often cries when she reads her bible.

Grandpa continues, "Now king snakes are speckled, and in some ways they look a lot like a rattler. But Charlie knew for sure this was a king because a' the shape a' his head. And while they usually stay away from people, why, here this one had clumb right up onto his porch. Charlie was right curious about the reason why. Of course, you can see why Bessie was a little nervous. But she waited on Charlie like he asked, and they watched that old boy as he paid them not so much as a howdy-do and turned towards their screen door."

Donnie Marie gulps. "Grandpa, he couldn't get in, could he? I mean the snake…I mean. What happened?"

"Well," says Grandpa, clicking his tongue against his teeth, "you see, Charlie was a little bit lax in takin' care of things. Oh he's a good farmer and all. Best cantaloupe in the county. But sometimes he let some of the house chores go a bit. And where our screen door fits nice and snug, well, Charlie's had a gap in it. A gap big enough for that snake to fit through. And that's exactly what he did."

"Did Mr. Porter get him then?"

"Believe me," he grins and straightens his back, "Bessie was surely losin' her patience by now. 'Charlie Porter, you'd better get that snake outta my house, or I'll go after him myself,' she told him.

"But Charlie was hooked now." And Grandpa chuckled. "'Just you wait, Bess,' he said. 'This old boy has something on his mind. I can feel it. Let's see what he's about.' So they followed, real quiet, followed that king snake right into the house, through the parlor, and into their very own bedroom. They watched him slip and slide up into the springs of their mattress, and suddenly there was a jumpin' and a hissin' and a rattlin'. That mattress had come alive!

"Bessie ran and got the gun and shoved it into Charlie's hands. 'Do somethin', do somethin'!' she yelled. Then all of a sudden, everything went still." Grandpa stops.

Reaching into his pocket he pulls out a piece of wood and begins to scrape with his knife. With a breathy whisper Donnie Marie asks, "What happened, Grandpa?"

Ginger moos in the barn. Old Joe and Eddie heehaw to each other as the pigs fill the sundown with their snorts and grunts.

Finally Grandpa stops his whittling and says, "Charlie tucked his gun under his elbow, pointing it with one arm, and reached out with the other one and turned the mattress over quick-like. There, wound up in the springs, was that king snake, his coils wrapped around a big ol' timber rattler, and he was swallowin' it down."

Donnie Marie's breathing was coming in short quick gasps, her eyes wide, her mouth forming a big O. Taking a big gulp of air she whispers, "Grandpa, you mean...?"

"That's right," he says. "Had Bessie and Charlie gone to bed that night that rattler would have surely kilt them both."

"Oh," she says, her breath escaping her body in a gust of air.

Grandpa works the wood for a minute or two, then says, "So that's why Charlie says he'll never kill a king snake to this very day. And that's why I say, some snakes are to be feared, and some are our friends."

Donnie Marie sits there. She looks out into the purple quiet of the evening. Fireflies are beginning to blink their secrets to one another. Grandma sits quietly, her mouth pinched in a funny kind of smile. Donnie Marie looks up at Grandpa with one eye closed.

"Is that really true, Grandpa? Did that really happen?"

"Why," Grandpa says, his eyes shiny as the stars, "would I lie?"

Celts

Kayleigh B. McKey

The rain was a drizzling mist, intertwining with the swirling fog that drifted through the dark valley. The trees and grass were silent in the breeze, stirring the deep scent of wet hay and the sea-smell of Irish moss. Birds whispered to each other above, waiting for their echo to return from the surrounding mountains.

Brennen was watching the birds and clenching his teeth at the absence of blue skies, at the continuous clouds, gray and black and morbid.

At the edge of the glen, the Celts stood quietly with their heads bowed. The only sounds were the whimpers of Posiella, the sniffling of Eoghan, and the suppressed sobs of Aibhilinn as Conri encircled her in his arms.

Rhiannon couldn't continue her prayer. Her voice had caught too many times already, and it was enough to watch as Morganna blessed the fragile body wrapped in satin. As Morganna whispered farewells in ancient Gaelic and placed herbs beside Aoife's form, Rhiannon's shoulders shook in torment. She had delivered this girl, when Aoife had been born. She had bathed her, fed her, cared for her, this one who now lay in an entrapping vessel and who was taking Morganna's prayers to the Otherworld as Morganna spoke.

Rhiannon dared to look at her family's faces, at those of the children she had delivered and helped raise, the Creations whom she loved like her own children, more than anything. They all looked old, shriveled and frail. Her children were older than herself now.

Morganna finished and stood after leaning over Aoife's body on its makeshift altar.

Every person there stood silently, not wanting to do the next part. Suddenly, Conri stepped forward, leaving Aibhilinn moaning and reaching for him. He kneeled at the feet of his daughter's body, prepared to lift the end. Slowly, Egan emerged from the group. His steps were very unsteady, though he attempted to plant his feet firmly. He would not fall to his knees now.

As he approached Conri and the body of Aoife, his throat tightened. Who would have known that he would have to see this day, that he wouldn't wake up one morning to see the beautiful girl leaning over him, smiling? He wouldn't see her standing on her tiptoes in the kitchen, trying to reach for a bowl up high in a cupboard. He wouldn't be able to watch out the bay window in the sunroom and see her riding her horse out in the pastures.

She was gone now, forever gone, no longer able to open her eyes to her mystical home or her loving family. They were closed for the rest of Earth's existence.

"...and may the Great Earth Mother always guide your gentle spirit wherever you go, my dear. The Sky Father will take you into his arms. May they protect you and guard you from harm."

Egan realized he had been standing over Aoife for a while, as his mind reunited with the present and the remembrance of Aoife's tragedy disturbed his wonderful reminiscence. The ancient voice of the goddess Morganna quieted to nothing, and now everyone shifted uncomfortably.

Rhiannon, seizing the courage and strength she needed, walked forward, her robes drifting over the grass. "As is custom," she began, her voice catching as it had earlier during her turn to speak, "Aoife will rest here for the Earth to depart and yet welcome her, and she will be buried at dawn." Rhiannon slowly retreated to her place beside Hephaestia, who gripped her hand tightly. She looked into her adopted daughter's bright green eyes that glimmered like the Irish Sea at morning. Tears spilled onto her cheeks, and she tried to smile at Rhiannon but broke into weeping instead.

Beside Hephaestia, Pryderi clasped her free hand, silent tears running down his face. He looked up at Nyk expectantly, letting loose his mother's hand and reaching up. Nyk, who had tears itching in his eyes, let them spill over as he picked up his son, holding him close to his chest.

Always cherish your children, Nyk, son of Nyx, a voice said in Nyk's head; you never know when the Sky Father will call upon their essence.

He turned and began walking down the slope towards the fields and Rhiannon's cottage. Noticing him leaving, Hephaestia followed her husband reluctantly, wiping her eyes of the sadness. Eventually, one by one, the Creations peeled away from the gravesite. As they left, no one speaking, Egan kneeled down across from Conri. Conri's hair, once light blonde, was now pale of color, and gray streaked it more than it had years ago. Egan sighed to keep himself from wailing out to the world, and he finally said to Conri, "Sir?"

Conri shook with tears, but calmed himself with Egan's voice. He looked up from the gently sheet-wrapped face of his daughter. "Yes," he whispered almost inaudibly.

Egan swallowed, not knowing how to approach the matter. This was the father of the only female creature that he would love in his whole existence, and yet he was asking so much, maybe too much, of Conri. Inhaling swiftly and attempting to control his breathing, Egan's voice cracked. "Conri, I would like to ask your permission to sit vigil this night with Aoife. I know that it is not nearly my place to even ask because you are the last man to have her in your care. But…"

Egan felt like he was rushing, and he looked at Aoife's body for help. His faltering voice suggested that maybe it was too much for him to handle rather than too much for Conri to allow.

Conri's words shocked Egan, and Egan's head shot up.

"Egan, I know you loved my daughter. Maybe more than anyone here ever did, including myself. I feel I was never cruel to you for it, but I also never acknowledged you, and the misery brought upon us is my way of paying for it." Pain crossed his face and his shoulders slumped under his over-tunic. "I would be more than honoured to let you sit vigil with my child."

At that moment, Egan realized how much he and Conri were alike. They would never be unfeeling. They were men, in flesh, with a heart and a soul and words. They knew loss now, even if they had experienced it together.

The two men lifted the straw carrier Aoife had been laid on and gently placed it on the ground beside the awaiting pile of stones. Conri stood then, passing a sad Morganna, who frowned at Egan.

"He will be fine, Aunt," Conri murmured to the goddess, caressing her long black hair. She held back tears and hesitantly followed her brother's Creation.

Egan coughed. He groaned, his stomach twisting like a horse with colic. A pain raked its hateful claws through his chest, penetrating his still-beating heart, like the knife wound that Aoife carried on her throat. He gasped for an abandoning breath, for an air far from where he slouched on Aoife's body. He cried, like Aoife had when she fell from the dragon's back as a child and broke her wrist.

He had been going to ask for her hand the coming spring.

He finally let loose the threatening tremors of pain, letting them course through his body until his shoulders and head throbbed. He remembered her soothing words, recalling them like yesterday.

He had been kneeling at their Uncle Pilib's newly filled grave, tears threatening his eyes. A soft hand rested on his shoulder, soothing his hate and distraction. All of a sudden, his grudge against the Saxons dissipated.

"It's okay to cry, Egan. It doesn't make you weak; it makes you the human you are. It's okay to cry."

The way she had said his name…her voice pulled at him like an unknown force. Only yesterday did it sing for him and whisper her innermost secrets.

Egan longed to feel her skin again, to know the feel of her hair, the freckles gracing her cheeks and nose, the folds of her léine dress.

He laid his head on her unmoving body, his ear listening to the silence within her. He lay down beside her, his hand resisting the urge to rip the satin and kiss her face. He wouldn't do that. She never told him of feeling the love for him that he felt for her. It was not his right to betray the friendship they had maintained to begin with. His best friend, and sometimes his only friend, was now gone from his embrace, but he couldn't take his mind from her.

"It's okay to cry, Egan."

Egan closed his eyes, tears sliding over his nose and onto the fabric.

He fell to sleep there, and he dreamed of her. He dreamed of what could have been, what he had wanted since childhood: to hold her in his arms for as long as they both breathed, to kiss her and smell her hair, and to give her children and grow old with her. He saw them both, holding hands and walking through the forests of Avalon. Children ran everywhere, and the dragons swooped above.

He dreamt of their childhood, Posiella and Caireann running ahead with the horses and other children. Aoife caught her breath and dropped into the grass, her Celtic woven gown billowing around her, her blonde curls hitching in the wind. Egan ran to her and sat beside her. They lay back and watched the clouds pass. She held his hand, and he held it to his chest.

She had asked him to promise her something: to be there for her forever. It became another pact to add to their other two: to be her slave and to be her best friend. With the double intersecting scars on each of their palms still trying to heal, they put a sharp stone to the tender flesh once more.

He had reached into the pocket of his breeches, pulling out a long string. On the end of it dangled a small Cross of Brighid made of willow. He placed it gently around her neck, smiling into the six-year-old's glowing eyes before bashfully saying, "Think of it as an early wedding gift." The words had spilled out before he could stop them, along with the quick kiss he gave her rosy cheek before she turned away.

His heart had fluttered. He stood still for a moment, watching her run and stumble to the Home of Rhiannon. He knew, at that moment, that despite Aoife's vague ignorance of true adulthood, he could await the thought of a home, the thought of the girl he treasured more than anything in all of Avalon becoming something of a beautiful young woman, marrying him, expecting him to make her happy, which he would certainly try to do.

He was happy, content with life. He was a ten-year-old boy with no imagination and no care in the world, as Aoife had always accused him before. But little did she know that she was very wrong indeed. She was the only friend he wanted, the only one he needed. And he looked forward to a forever with his best friend, a little piece of an eternity with Aoife and Avalon and Pilib and the dragons.

Young Aoife turned back to him, her gown flowing in the tall grass, her smile warming. "Egan."

"Egan. Wake up."

The voice changed, and instantly, Egan knew that something wasn't right.

As someone gently shook his shoulder and repeated his name, his eyes fluttered open and he recognized the voice as Faolan's—older, deeper than Aiofe's.

Egan wasn't ten years old anymore.

He looked around, confused until he realized where he was. Aoife's body, still wrapped in the satin, lay under his head and he looked up to see Faolan kneeling beside him.

"Egan, wake up. It's dawn."

Egan rose slowly to a sitting position, his eyelids heavy with realization. "Where is everyone?" he whispered.

Faolan's naturally grave face was quieter this morning, and his voice was soft with sorrow. "They are all at

Rhiannon's Home. Aibhilinn is at our cottage. She was feeling ill this morning."

Egan looked down once more at Aoife's face, the curves of her lips and nose visible through the cloth. "Tell them that I will be down shortly."

Faolan nodded. "Very well." When he stood, he realized he couldn't step away. He swallowed the salty bile building in his throat, and his voice was hollow. "Thank you for loving my sister, Egan."

Egan turned his head slightly and gave a brief nod. Faolan turned away from the tree line and his friend, his long dark cloak wrapping around his ankles, and walked back into the knee-high grass towards Rhiannon's cottage.

Egan straightened and got to his knees, feeling that Faolan was far enough away. Reaching up to the nape of his neck, he untied the string underneath his unshorn brown curls. Bringing his hands in front of him, he eased the pendent from under his coat and tunic. It hung in the air, and he watched St. Brighid's cross carved from willow swing endlessly.

Only yesterday he had found it on her body when she was brought back, but it seemed like ages ago that he let it lie on his chest, millennia ago.

Egan traced his thumb over it gently, loving the feel of the soft wood. He wound the string of the necklace numerously around his hand and laid the fist he made on Aoife's chest. He lightly placed his other hand on the side of Aoife's fragile face. At least he could imagine.

Bending over, he brushed his lips lightly against her satin-covered mouth. She seemed so cold, so lifeless.

Egan held his face to hers for a lifetime, willing her heart to beat at his touch. He unfurled his fist on her chest, letting the cross of Brighid slide from his fingers. It lay on the unmoving body, the cross as cold as Aoife's skin.

Egan leaned back reluctantly, and he brushed nonexistent hair from her face. "It was always yours to keep, my love," he murmured.

His legs shook as he rose to his feet, and his arms hung limply. The brooch at his throat that held his cloak together over his shoulders was almost choking him, and he adjusted it before stepping back.

There was a quiet brush through the grass behind Egan, but he didn't move. He only continued to stare at the pile of large stones beside Aoife.

The dragon stepped closer, his wings ruffling in the slight breeze that filled the glowing gray valley. He hung his long head over Egan's shoulder, sighing a breath of cold air.

Egan reached up and patted the animal's scarred snout. "I know, Great One. I know."

They walked to Rhiannon's cottage together, Egan's hand resting on the dragon's scaly side.

Currents

Heather Murphy

After dinner, Bridie waits on her bed, behind her mosquito netting, pretending to read a book. She waits to hear the sliding door, her parents' voices through the tiny window, then jumps up, heart pounding a rhythm of elated panic, and runs to their room. She sits on the edge of the unmade bed with the change jar, her hands clammy with theft and the tropical heat. She has never stolen anything in her life. She is twelve years old. She has already foreseen the consequences this act of treachery will set into motion when her parents discover that she is a thief, but she pushes past it, like rough waves close to the shore. *And he walks right out into the surf in his school clothes.*

The drawn-out sound of insect song fills her head, swarms in the air around her in the little room next to the blue Sea-That-Makes-No-Sound, *where he easily pushes past the first breakers.* A little thrill runs through her, like an electrical current, as she pictures his face, the joy he will feel, when she returns from Kapaa with three different kinds of cakes from the Safeway in the basket of her bicycle. *The deep, teal waves roll him about, like candy on a tongue. He thinks of a book his mother read to him once, about a boy who lived alone in the mountains with just a knife and some twine.*

She wipes at the sweat on her forehead, roughly pulls her blond hair back into a ponytail, then takes a deep breath and slowly pours the heavy change into the hammock of her dress-folds, *he is just floating, letting the current decide,* letting the coins slide across her hand and down her fingers, tilting her head to the side to see how they shine like moonlight playing on the waves. She marvels at the number of quarters, almost startled at how few pennies there are, and a feeling of richness washes over her. *And a new set of breakers meets him. There is a boat in the distance. It pushes into the sky.* She immediately pictures herself alone with two giant bags of chips—one corn with nacho cheese, the other, onion-flavored potato chips, roosting in her favorite ironwood tree down at the bay and *not* sharing them with Surrender. She quickly decides she is still angry with him for lying to the tourists, telling them he's from another island, even though he's Indian, from India, which is nowhere near Kauai. *He turns to regard the land with a detached calm, how the stump on the shore is now like a little spider on a railing.* She's angry with him for hating his life when that could only mean that she is not enough to make him happy.

"So what if I did?" He'd been defensive. Broody. Kicking at coconut husks.

"So, it's a big fat lie. Lies poison you, and you're from Connecticut, anyway," she'd reminded him. The sting of having no similar ruse, no disguise or novelty status, left a little barb. "You can't escape who you are," she'd said, mimicking her mother, Cordelia.

"You sound just like Cordelia," and then they had argued. He'd called her "brainwashed," and she'd told him that everyone thought his parents were weirdos for being white Hindus while their adopted son was an Indian atheist.

"I can say I am from anywhere, if it's just a game to me. Maybe I'll go to another island and then I can say, 'Hey people, I'm from another island,' and it'll be true," he'd said, staring off into nothing.

"What'll you do, swim out in the Sea-That-Makes-No-Sound and have a turtle pick you up and give you a ride to a place where no one knows you?" she had asked, laughing, but she didn't like the sound of his voice, and little alarm bells had sounded off, somewhere inside her.

"Why do you still call it that?" he'd sneered, making her face go hot. When they were very small and met for the first time, he said, "You're just little, so I'll have to name everything for you," and she'd pointed to the thick line of their bay, and he'd puffed up with importance to inform her that *that* was a magical place called, "The-Sea-That-Makes-No-Sound."

"I still call it that because that's its secret name."

"You're younger than me; you don't understand what it's like. You don't even have to go to school. You're, like, sheltered from all this shit. Maybe I want to go where there aren't any stupid people asking me where I'm from." And he'd unwrapped a Kashi bar, not offering her any, even frowning at a little red-crested cardinal that walked over, when usually, he would break a piece off and toss it. The bird had walked away, dejected, and a heavy feeling had come to her chest, like someone had placed a stone in her rib cage.

"A year, and a few months—big deal. Cordelia says girls mature faster, plus I've read more books. I am actually older than you."

Surrender didn't laugh or smile at her line of reasoning or roll his eyes as he usually did. Instead, he'd said he hated his life, but the words were muttered. She'd left him and walked all the way to the tourist trap to stalk about with the useless Givenchy wallet her aunt had sent her, pretending *she* was from somewhere else, until the angry Thai lady who wore too much perfume realized the wallet was probably empty and shooed her out.

Bridie remembers the time Surrender pulled her from the grasp of a wave, the time he got her down from a little breadfruit tree when she was too frightened to move, the time he brought back coconut cake from a luau his rich grandparents from Boston took him to when they visited three months ago, the only fancy luau either of them had ever been to. How he had unwrapped it so carefully. How his face had transformed as soon as it hit his lips, and how she had feigned awe at the taste, to make this most sacrosanct of rituals more meaningful for him, when really, she hated coconut cake. *The water seems to grow still as dusk begins to gather across the expanse of sky. He floats on his back for a moment, picturing Bridie's face when she finds out he has drowned, trying to swim to Niihau.*

A wave of pity comes over her, and she fills the fancy wallet with coins. She wants only to see him as he was when they had the cake, down by the bay that night, when he would never be so selfish as to buy chips and eat them in secret. Surrender is forbidden to eat junk food and only eats food deemed "satvic" by his mother, which means it doesn't have sugar or chemicals and nobody lost their temper while preparing it. *The sheer folly of his plan becomes obvious as the moon begins its ascent and the pink clouds lose their color.*

She makes the dangerous trip up Route 56 to the Safeway in record time, arriving at dusk *he has to fight a little now* and goes straight back to the bakery, where the packaged squares of cakes with icing are, and picks out three, *he has to swim hard and he is tired* paying for them with the change, not making eye contact with the clerk, and just as darkness falls, she arrives back and gathers up the cakes, *he can just make out Bridie's favorite tree* throws the bike down, and makes her way down to the bay, where she sits under the ironwood tree to wait for him to sneak out of his house.

A feeling of happiness comes over her as she stares out at the sea, at the shimmering path the moon's light lays down on the water, a path that leads to a brilliant sheet of the brightest white light Surrender used to call "The Moon Room" when they were kids. And as she's gazing out, a form begins to take shape there and come closer, and she absently wonders what it is, as she realizes she didn't get forks and they'll have to eat the cake with their hands.

Leaving My Broken House
John Richard Sack

The haibun *is a literary form that balances prose and haiku poetry (in both its regular and irregular forms). The classic examples of this joined form are the poet Matsuo Bashō's travel notes, written in the late 1600s. See, for example,* The Narrow Road to the Deep North and Other Travel Sketches *(Penguin Books, 1966), in which Bashō describes not only the landscapes, shrines, and people he met along the way, but also the spiritual pilgrimage advancing simultaneously within him. Referring to Komon (Kuang-wên), a Chinese priest of the Nansung dynasty, he wrote:*

> *Following the example of the ancient priest who is said to have traveled thousands of miles caring naught for his provisions and attaining the state of sheer ecstasy under the pure beams of the moon, I left my broken house on the River Sumida …*

In this same spirit, Saku-jin (Evolving Man), following his awakening 300 years later, wandered through southern Oregon, a region nostalgically similar in its seasons and rugged topography to his beloved Japan. In Leaving My Broken House, *he records the opening year of his travels. The following excerpt, "Winter," is the first of the four seasons described in his journal. The full version of* Leaving My Broken House *will be available through Amazon and other sources by spring 2016.*

Winter

In the midst of a rainy winter I find myself on the edge of the western world—a beach below Cape Blanco, Oregon. The southwest wind vents its fury on this unprotected stretch of coast. The ocean bellows and churns with foam, a chant and dance it has practiced for a thousand ages, but all its fierce ritual ends in delicate sprays curling across the sand. Here, where the land begins and ends, I've set out this New Year's Day.

The masters say each place in every instant is where we start, in a universe renewed at every moment. The sunrise is hidden this specific instant in shrouds of cloud and vapor rising from the tops of evergreens. The heavy air mutes even the gulls. They wheel ghost-like through the fog, seekers like me, although perhaps more certain of their goal.

> I greet the New Year.
> Groping down an unknown road
> In my pilgrim's robe.

> Waves scour the sand—
> A clean slate
> This New Year's Day.

I admire the ancient trees, gnarled gargantuan bonsai, tenacious in their grip on the sculpted cliffs. Some have finally surrendered and let go their hold on the rocks. Air currents moan through the cavities of rotted trunks, improvising preternatural sea songs.

Tall firs lean like wheat
Before they lunge, uprooted,
To the earth's embrace.

Wind currents mimic
The ageless hymn of the whale
Through hollowed trunks.

Turning my back to the gusts, I let them push me up the path to a battered lighthouse. The building is locked, but on its lee side I gain brief protection from the weather.

The rains, from downpour to drizzle, are constant in these dark months of the coastal year. Confusion and a sense of something lacking—a soul turned inside out by cabin fever —have forced me from my home and stove. With rain gear, tent, pack, and walking staff as my sole supplies, I shut my cottage door and began this sojourn of the soul.

Quitting his broken home,
He launched into the somber
Drift of winter.

I long at once for a wise and experienced guide, for I've no idea where this journey will lead. A verse from the *Zenrinkushu* reminds me:

If you wish to know the road up the mountain,
You must ask the man who goes back and forth on it.

Will I return with snow-white hair, brilliant as the crown of Shasta's sacred mountain? Will I return at all? Many of the old ones died while on the road, trekking to eternity.

I find a trail that winds uphill to an inland slough. Here, the gusts are calmer with the cape and trees behind me as a windbreak. The marsh appears deserted, serene in its mantle of mist. By some such pond, Matsuo Bashō heard a frog kerplunk, opening a portal to the other world.

> *Furuike ya kawazu tobikomu mizu no oto.*
> Breaking the silence
> Of an ancient pond,
> A frog jumped into water—
> Deep resonance.

Deep resonance, indeed, if we focus on its source. Don't be distracted by the ripples!

Does one always waken to Reality with a start, like Bashō in this poem, like Saul of Tarsus tumbling sightless from his horse? Or do such moments sneak upon us, softly stirring us from sleep? Is the Spirit ever groaning, begging graces for us even as we languish unaware? If I abide awhile in silence, this pool may burble up an answer from its murky depths.

> Soft rain nourishes
> The willow's thirsty roots,
> Despite the dark night.

But then the startling to awareness—

Drowsy morning fog
Shrouds the silent slough
Thunder of heron wings!

Who is more startled, the bird or I? I am almost beside it when it lifts off a stump at the water's edge. In the custom of the native people of this coast, I, months before, had recognized the Great Blue Heron as my spirit guide. This sign, at the very outset of my pilgrimage, is auspicious. At once, it seems, the sky lightens and the wind and rain abate. With a word of thanks for an unexpected blessing, I continue up the hill.

Beside a rutted, muddy road, I am hailed from a truck splashing in my direction. "Look at that!" the driver shouts, jerking backwards with his thumb. "I hauled him from New River not ten minutes ago. Took an hour to land." The fish is huge, a sturgeon long as the rusted truck bed. "I'm taking it to town, to get its picture in the paper."

He offers me a ride. I remind myself that teachers are everywhere and each meeting is a chance to learn. I gratefully accept the lift. We pass a crossroads market, and he tells me that he cooks for income, strums guitar for joy, and sings in the restaurant when the last meal's served. "Chef Jeff the Music Man." He lives alone by choice, admits he's prone to wanderlust, and is always glad to help a fellow nomad.

My good angel cooks me breakfast—mushrooms, coffee, eggs and toast—at his cafe. His home is Bandon-by-the-Sea, a village at the mouth of the Coquille River. He asks me for a poem as payment for my breakfast, and I scrawl upon a napkin:

The cafe singer
Could compose a ballad:
"Pickup Full of Fish."

Sleepy patrons stumble in for their first coffee of the day. In a corner, fishermen debate the safety of the bar where the river meets the sea. I feel a sudden sorrow for the men and boats this town has lost and for their widows grieving on the shore. I pray this gusty morning that these men will turn back home to celebrate the New Year with their families.

His trawler foundered
On the bar. The fish and he
Now sleep more deeply.

I thank my host again and wander to a dock near the cafe. At this early hour I find a solitary man seated at the end of the pier, meditating as the ripples whisper underneath. Stolid as a mountain, he pays no heed to the drizzle. Between us is a maze of pottery and garden figurines.

A glaze of raindrops
Fills Saint Francis' folded arms
To form a birdbath.

He ends his morning practice and flips a small stone into the lapping water. When he sees me watching, he explains, "Each day I drop a pebble in the river, here below the pier where it's ten feet deep. By the time my rock pile breaks the surface, I hope to have made some bit of progress." He goes his way, saying he has urns to fire before he opens shop. I nod to this patient tutor and take the plank seat he has just vacated. One must surely gain from sitting in a space so hallowed by daily dedication. I toss a stone into the water when I finally rise to go.

After noon I cross the Coquille River bridge, following the highway signs to Bullard's Beach. The park is empty this midwinter day, and I raise my dome tent in a grove of sheltering pines. Misshapen boughs curve over and around it like the broken stones of a cenobite's cell. The branches serve as my umbrella and remind me of a former meditation site, a bench within a copse of birches. The trees there leaned beside a pond, where the single resident koi rose to the surface to inspect me. Her gaze and manner led me to believe she was an old soul, and I returned her greeting with a reverential bow.

> Golden mother koi,
> Will you teach me how
> To see as you do?

I wonder whether I might, in this private sanctuary, wait out the rains for several days before I leave again. My answer comes next morning when the ranger wakes me, calling from outside my tent. His name is Anders, and after I explain my plan, he leads me to his manufactured home for breakfast. He tells me that the park in winter has few visitors and gets busy only when the schools begin their April break. If I will help prepare the campsites for these next few months, he will let me stay in one of the park's several yurts, wait out the winter in this solitary place, and resume my journey when the wind shifts to the north. The wind shift spells the end of winter on the coast, the beginning of its only other season: the chill spring-summer-autumn months of morning fog and stiff north winds. Outside Anders' window, white-tailed does meander through the pines as we shake hands on the deal.

> Two men talk at dawn,
> With naught but steaming coffee
> Raised between them.

Rising each day in my luxurious yurt, I confess I am embarrassed to think of the tiny hermitage of the priest Bucchō behind Unganji Temple. Bashō described it:

> Less than five feet square,
> My thatched cottage;
> I would gladly quit even this
> But for the rain.

Ah, but for the rain....

I begin each morning giving thanks for this astounding gift. When the day is dry, I sit upon a flat rock, part of a jetty that protects another vacant lighthouse. I see the potter on his dock, a speck on the opposite shore, and thus our morning meditations span the river. In a country so devoid of shrines, people must create their own.

> I bow below
> This empty, darkened lighthouse,
> Awakening to Light.Shadows shifting on
> The far side of the river.
> What lies hidden there?

In my daily round of service in the campground, I pick up storm debris and fallen limbs, saw broken pine and cedar branches into stacks of firewood for the summer and seal wounded trees with a tarry pitch. I also clean the campsites used by rare winter visitors. At noon I cross the bridge into the village, buy groceries, and eat my main meal of the day. By evening I am on my stone ledge once again, watching the cormorants skim the river, fishing by twilight, disappearing into the dimming water when they spot a meal.

Back inside my yurt by nightfall, often with the rain drumming on the roof, I think of Lu Yün's "Valley Wind."

> Living in retirement beyond the world,
> silently enjoying my isolation,
> I pull the rope of my door tighter
> and stuff my window with roots and ferns.
> My spirit is attuned to the spring season.
> At the fall of the year there is autumn in my heart.
> Thus imitating cosmic changes
> my hut becomes a universe.

I bow to his genius, kindle a fire in the woodstove, and write a linked reply straddling the centuries and miles between us:

> Monsoons pound my hut.
> Flickers of cedar embers
> Gild my naked walls.

The seasonal change is coming soon and, like Yu, I tune my spirit to greet it:

Ice on the inlets;
Fish, motionless beneath it,
Share a dream of spring.

A Perfect Day

Barbara Summerhawk

"Hi, Teri! Beautiful day, isn't it?" Ken hopped out of his pickup in Teri's gravel driveway, parking just under the cherry tree fully leafed out.

"Hi, Ken. Good to see you." They give each other a conventional hug.

"How've you been, Ken?"

"Good, T. You?"

"Too good."

"Huh?"

"Have you noticed anything peculiar lately?"

"About what?"

"Life. I mean here. Life."

"Life?"

"Just life, here in the valley." They walk over and lean against the corral fence.

"I don't know what you mean."

"It's too perfect."

"Yeah?"

"I mean, if we want to fly and we go to top launch, there's always the perfect breeze and we fly as long as we want."

"So?"

"So, no one's had any incidents or accidents in how long?"

"Well, that's a good thing, don't you think?"

"Ordinarily, but…it's just strange."

"Why?"

"Consider another example. You went fishing last week, right?"

"Yeah, so?"

"You caught just the right number for dinner and under the limit, in just the right amount of time on the river. Your words."

"Hmm."

"And it's the middle of summer, yet it rains at night two or three times a week. There's no real fire danger. Usually, forest fires are popping up everywhere."

"Luck of the weather, I suppose." Ken kicks his boot at a piece of gravel.

"Let me ask you another question: when was the last time you left the valley?"

"Well, I went into Ashland last week to pick up some groceries at the Co-op. Other than that, I don't really want to leave the valley. Everything is here."

"Do you remember the getting there? I mean, do you remember the trip, passing through Jacksonville, the stoplights, the store parking lot, anything?"

"Come to think of it, no. I do remember leaving the house, driving past Ruch.... Then I was driving back with the groceries."

"Don't you find that odd?" Teri asked.

"A little. Maybe I just spaced it all." Ken shrugged.

"The whole two or three hours that would take?"
Silence.

"Well, I call people. I get emails from everyone. I think you're making too much of our good luck this summer."

"Okay. Go ahead. Call someone in Medford."

"All right. I'll call Mel, and check if he's coming out this way anytime soon. He's got his old place up here on Humbug."

"Yeah, ask him if you can stop in on Tuesday."

"Why Tuesday?"

"Just do it."

Ken dials Mel's number. Answering machine.

"All right, so he's not home." Ken shrugs.

"Try Sheila."

He dials. Answering machine.

"Well, sooner or later they gotta be home."

"Maybe."

"What are you getting at?"

"I'm not sure." Teri pauses and a slight frown dawns. "Don't get me wrong," she says. "It's a beautiful summer." Pause. "But what if, from now on, that's all it is?"

"I never know what you're talking about." Ken's frustration shows in his voice. "You take a few unusual coincidences and make some kind of conspiracy puzzle out of them."

"Oh, maybe." Teri walks over to the fence. "It's just too perfect. Something's a little off." She leans against the fence, then turns back to Ken.

"Look, I can't recall when I went to pick up hay for the horses, but the barn's still full. Things like that."

"Whew. You scared me there for a minute." Ken wipes his brow in faux relief. "An endless supply of horse fodder. Gosh. Jon Stewart would be happy."

"Ha, ha."

"No, really. Why be unhappy about comfort? You don't have to take the truck to Tim's and load and unload hay, at least for awhile."

"It's just… weird. In a way, we can only live with what we have at the moment."

"Well, you do zen. Maybe you finally reached *satori*."

"It's not like that."

"What?"

"It's… this… I'm pretty sure it isn't *satori*."

"You're the Buddhist, not me. I still say it's just an unusually perfect run of good fortune."

"What if it's not?"

"Well, so, what if it's not?" Ken kicks the gravel with his boot again. "Look, I stopped by to get my weed whacker back. I'd like to trim down around the ditch along the road in front of my house. You finished with it?"

"Yeah, I am. As a matter of fact, I probably won't need to borrow it again." Teri walks towards the barn with Ken following.

"It's August. The dry heat will just about kill anything."

"About that…" Teri grabs the weed whacker from in front of some bales of hay and hands it to Ken.

"Now what? August heat a part of the conspiracy?" He grasps the weed whacker, turns it upside down, and inspects the motor.

"Haven't you noticed the weather? Tell me, how hot is it right now?"

"Hmm, I'd say in the 80s."

"Yeah. Yesterday it was August 19 and it was 75."

"Pleasant."

"Weird."

"Why? Like I said…"

"No, it's more than weird. We haven't had any super hot, 'August Dog Days' yet this summer."

"For once, global warming works in our favor?" They are walking to Ken's blue Toyota truck.

"Perfectly, if you ask me."

"Geez and so what?" Ken says. "What if this is what we have to live with forever? Can't you be happy about that?"

"If I didn't know you better, I'd think you were part of the conspiracy."

"This ain't the 'Truman Show,' Teri. I don't know why things are good right now, but I'm not going to worry about it."

"Wouldn't you like to know why? Who's pulling the strings?"

"God."

"You don't believe in Her."

"Fate. Karma. Random wind patterns. I gotta go."

"Okay, maybe it's nothing, but if it does amount to something, why us? What do you have to do? You're in such a hurry."

"Nothing much. Can we change the subject?"

"Time for tea?"

"Okay. One cup. But no more on the perfect valley." They go into Teri's house and Ken sits at the counter while Teri puts on the kettle. She turns from the stove and leans on the counter to Ken's side.

"So have you seen Norma lately?" she asks.

"No, not for a few weeks. I ask her to come out here, but she's always got something going on." He shakes his head. "Never been busier, it seems."

"She can't get out here." Teri pours hot water into the cups she's set up and puts the sugar and milk up on the counter.

"Now don't start." Ken says in slightly too-loud a voice.

"Okay. Okay. I was wondering if you two were, you know, getting more serious."

"Yeah, well, I'd kinda like that, but I wouldn't want to move into Medford, and she doesn't exactly feel about the valley the same way I do."

"I see." Teri nods slowly, as if preoccupied.

"Teri, you're pushing this conspiracy thing too far."

"Well, what if it is only us?" she asks suddenly. Then she pauses and takes a sip of tea. "All of us here. In the valley. Who love the valley. Tell me, if you envision a perfect day here, wouldn't it look like today?"

"Hmm. Yeah, I suppose."

"What if we all reached that feeling one day at the exact same time, all of us, consciously wishing for the perfect August?"

"What?"

"The question is, do we want to stay with this?"

"Well. Who wouldn't? Listen, I'm going to go." He takes another gulp of tea and stands up, moving to the door.

"Thanks for the tea, T." His old standby joke line.

"No problem, Ken." She walks him to his truck. He gets in.

"Ken..."

"What?"

"You can go to Medford anytime you really want to."

"I know that."

"No, I mean, you'd have to leave the valley."

"Teri, take some time off." He starts the engine and backs out of the driveway. He waves good-bye.

Teri stands there a minute and returns to the house, picks up the phone and dials a California number.

"Debbie. Hi. It's Teri," she says into the receiver.

"Fine," she continues. "Say, listen, you know how you're always talking about moving up to the valley? Why don't you come up this weekend and just chat?" Teri listens, then smiles. "Good. Yes, Saturday is fine…."

My Grandmother's Necklace

Marilyn Terry

Some time ago I opened my grandmother's jewelry box, and inside it I discovered a lovely necklace. This story is to tell exactly what happened afterwards.

You will never believe it! No! Never! Not ever! But this is the exact truth!

Above is a sketch of my grandmother when she was young.

First of all, the necklace was *much* admired by my Scottish deerhounds, Gaelic, Bronwen, Edal, Bumbles, and Rowan. And by Galina, my very naughty Siberian husky. They gazed awestruck at the gorgeous necklace with wide eyes. Galina was particularly fascinated. Her beady eyes were glommed on to the necklace's equally beady beads, while all sorts of devilish thoughts spun through her mind.

"Ooh! It is so lovely!" Gaelic sighed longingly. She wanted it for herself but was much too polite to say so.

"That necklace is *so* beautiful!" thought Edal wistfully. "It reminds me of all the scents and colours of Scotland! If *only* I owned a necklace like that!"

"I *want* that!" Galina rudely exclaimed with sudden energy, interrupting everyone's reverie. "*Right now!*"

She swiftly leapt up to seize the necklace. Just as swiftly I raised my hand to snatch it out of the way of her open mouth full of gleaming ivory teeth!

My older huskies, Olga, Xenia, Grimm, and Saski, were busy outside, frenziedly digging preposterously humongous holes in the soft dirt. Clods of earth and grass were flying everywhere.

What fun they were having, they thought!

What a mess they were making of my lawn, I thought!

However, they all stopped when they saw me with my newfound bead necklace, and they also much admired it. They *all* wanted it! They zoomed around me so furiously while trying to snatch it out of my hands that I became giddy. They were bouncing high in the air and grabbing madly, so I had to leave quickly and sit down, since my head was whirling and the ground was spinning so fast I was afraid I would fall down.

After I recovered a little by sitting at the picnic table with a cup of tea, I put the necklace around my neck for safety and decided to walk to the field to show my beautiful find to my horses.

Cancion and Gemaya were very polite. They softly sniffed the necklace around my neck while making very approving snuffly horsey sounds. Isabelle, my Welsh pony, eyed the necklace with all sorts of rascally notions flashing through her busy brain.

She was *not* so polite. She reached forward with her wicked whiskery muzzle, I thought to investigate my beautiful necklace. But no. Her teeth latched onto the bead necklace, and with a swift toss of her head it was torn from around my neck.

Off she trotted at a brisk pace, her impish Welsh head in the air, looking back at me, her mischievous bright eyes shining triumphantly. She appeared very pleased with herself.

In her clenched teeth my necklace was waving in the wind.

Naughty,

naughty

Isabelle!!

I stood dumbfounded! Cancion and Gemaya were equally astonished. We watched as Isabelle disappeared into the distance. I thought my necklace was gone forever. All the dogs, tails wagging and waving, were gaping at the drama from the opposite side of the fence with great keenness. The Huskies even thought this was much more fun than digging huge holes in my once-lovely lawn. "Open the gate!" they howled. "We will catch her for you!" they lied.

Munnings, my other Welsh pony, was also watching, but from afar. Munnings had recently left his previous life at a very advanced age to reside in the distant mystical island of Tir na nOg. He was thirty-two years old when he left here, but in the land of Tir na nOg he became young again, for this was the place of eternal youth, where beauty, health, and happiness last without end. Now he could forever enjoy life, grazing the lush green grass beside rippling streams, warmed by balmy sun and gentle clouds in the company of all the other good ponies and creatures who had gone before him. However, this day his thoughts were not so gentle as he observed Isabelle's shenanigans, for, you see, he could watch anything in any part of our planet from where he was living.

He raised his head and his bright shiny mane tossed in the breeze. He snorted violently, and he pounded the earth with his strong front foot.

BOOM!
BANG! BRANG! Pow!
and more POW!!

In an instant thunder roared earsplittingly; lightning flashed brightly. The earth shook and tossed on her moorings. The lights of the stars blinked out. The moon shut her eyes. A raging, rampaging, roaring storm howled and rattled in all its fuming, fierce, and fearsome fury. Leaden clouds scudded across the heavens, all in an abominably bad humor; the skies darkened to deepest, dismal, formidable, ominous, inkiest blackness. Sheeting rain began to fall in tumultuous torrents. Soon there was so much water that the creeks filled up and flash floods raced across the landscape.

"The world is coming to an end!" wailed Bronwen.

In no time at all we all became incredibly, miserably wet.

Munnings looked on aghast. "Goodness, woodness! Goodness, woodness!" was all he could whisper over and over as he stood in awe. "I didn't do that, did I? No, surely not!"

All who knew him knew Munnings as a very gentle pony who meant no harm in any way. No mean thought ever entered his head because he loved everyone (although those who knew him also remember some rather interesting moments when Munnings decided to take matters into his own hands—or should we say, his own hoofs).

"Yes you did!" cheerfully observed another chubby, chunky Tir na nOg pony with bright brown eyes enhanced by long lashes, who took the time to raise her head from her eating. Thick clumps of luscious green grass hung out of her mouth. "Yes, you most certainly did do that!"

"Oh dear!" mumbled Munnings contritely. "Oh dear!"

Meanwhile Isabelle careened to a sliding stop, startled by the booming of the thunder, the drenching rain, the sudden darkness, a turn of events she had never before experienced. She reared and bucked as the cascading downpour splashed on her hair and stung like icy, spiky needles into her skin. She didn't like that at all and she was *most* unhappy!

Isabelle is extremely cross!
She is having a horrible, gargantuan temper tantrum!

"I made a great big awful mistake," thought Isabelle.

She wheeled around, galloping as fast as she could, back to her barn and safety, the necklace still clamped in her teeth. When she reached me, she skidded to a sudden halt and opened her mouth with relief. The bead necklace fell onto the wet earth. She appeared very ashamed of herself. She shook herself vigorously, and a shower of rain danced in the air and landed on me, so I was drenched all over again! As I leant forward to pick up the necklace, she dropped her head to the ground, picked up the necklace herself, and gave it back to me. She told me she was very sorry and she would *never* do anything so naughty ever, ever again.

"Never, never!" she said.

"Hmmm!" I thought doubtfully.

Suddenly the rain stopped, and the wind ceased its roaring. The skies turned brilliant bright blue; the clouds billowed, dazzling white like luminous thunderheads. The sun came out, warm and golden, and the waters in all the creeks lowered as they raced toward the sea.

All the dogs and horses shook themselves and whoofed and whinnied gratefully. They all had words to say to Isabelle but decided to wait until another time because, after all, she had given everyone a jolly good rip-roaring show.

Of course, we know Isabelle will soon forget her good intentions.

And Munnings smiled to himself.

And I have my necklace back.

And everyone was so worn out that everyone fell asleep.

The following is a scene from a novel in progress by this author.

Fire Lily
Christin Lore Weber

Laylah's Grandpa Johann used to read the story about the fire lily backwards from the last page to the first. "Grandpa!" she'd correct him, exasperated, "start at the beginning," and he'd laugh, calling her angel-girl. She showed him the page, the correct page. Dear Grandpa. He'd do it right, then, while she straddled the back of the leather easy chair and let her fingers wander along the paths in his sparse gray hair.

Another little stroke, her momma called his trouble. Then another, and his right hand turned to ice. Thumb and forefinger stuck together, and the other three fingers cleaved to his palm. "Help me, angel," he said as he tried to lift a dining room chair, tried to slide a wooden slat between that frozen finger and that thumb. Days of trying, weeks, maybe. When he accomplished the feat, the two of them danced a little jig. "You silly man," Granny Marta called from the kitchen. "Next thing you'll take a tumble, and it'll be the death of you."

Six strokes, seven, and Granny Marta along with Momma and Daddy put him in his bed in the back room where the clock marked the hours and Grandpa repeated *"Gesu, Maria, Josef"* with each chime. Laylah sat at the foot of the bed and sang to him, *Jesus, Jesus, come to me,* from her First Communion Day. Father Bonaventure arrived with candles, holy water, oils, and prayers to trace crosses on Grandpa's hands that worked good deeds, on feet that took him on journeys of mercy, on lips that comforted and prayed, on ears that heard the word of God, on eyes that looked upon the world with love. "Where's my girl?" Grandpa said right in the middle of it all just like he didn't know a holy thing was going on. "Where's my little angel?"

"I'm right here." She started to climb onto the bed. Then Granny hushed her. Everyone else was kneeling, the whole family except for Uncle Adam, who didn't hold with religious ceremony and had curled his big body into the overstuffed leather chair in the corner of the front room. He held his puffy hands over his ears and moaned, "Dad, Dad, Dad, Dad." The priest looked up from his blessings and said, "It's okay, Laylah," which overrode Granny Marta's hush, and Laylah crawled to Grandpa's side to snuggle against him.

She got used to him being that way. She got used to the big wooden chair by the side of the bed with a potty underneath. She got used to his mumbling. Maybe she thought all of this would just continue from then on. She stopped by to see him every day after school, beginning to anticipate their visit by afternoon recess and then running to Granny Marta's, where he'd still be in the same place, still repeating his mantra.

One Friday her momma called the school to have Laylah's teacher tell her she'd be staying with her friend Glenna overnight. Glenna, a year older than Laylah, would stop by the third-grade classroom after school to pick her up, and they would get a ride home with Glenna's mom. It was December with a blizzard blowing in from Canada across Lake of the Woods. Momma would be staying with Granny Marta. Laylah would have fun playing with Glenna. That was the message. Laylah wasn't sure. Why couldn't she talk to her

FROM THE HEART OF THE APPLEGATE

mother? But the whole thing was clear. It was simple. Just go to Glenna's house. That's all.

It would be simple but for Glenna's dad, a stern man with a bony face and skim milk eyes who also was the town doctor. The first time Laylah ever saw him, way back when she was just a little kid of four, she burst into tears. She wasn't even sick, and he wasn't in his clinic but at a party. Her mother had dressed her up in a creamy satin dress to show her off, but when she saw Glenna's dad she screamed no, no, no, then burst into tears. "What's wrong? What is it?" Her mother bent over her. No, no, no, no! It was angles. It was gold rims on glasses. It was eyes without color. It was a stick man, bone man, nightmare man. Fear rushed up electric from heart to throat and out her arms, her fingers, down her legs. "Momma, Momma," she sobbed. "NO!"

"What's wrong? It's just Dr. Hall."

She was older by several birthdays on that Friday she was sent home with Glenna, but the thought of the doctor still jolted her. She could hide from him, she thought. It was a big house. Four houses like her own could fit inside Glenna Hall's big house.

Wind whooshed through the backyard cedars, and sleet clicked against the windows of Glenna's room. The girls hid all Glenna's dolls under her mom's red satin comforter to keep them safe and then cuddled in beside them. "We'll tell them stories so they won't be afraid," Glenna said. Light from the room slid under the comforter's edges. A strangeness crept around Laylah's heart and seeped into her belly, but she didn't know what it was. Then they heard Mrs. Hall's voice from the direction of the bedroom door.

"I've been looking all over for you girls," she said as she pulled the comforter off the whole bunch of them. "Laylah? Will you come down to the living room with me? Dr. Hall wants to have a word with you."

There remained no memory of going down the stairs. There remained only the memory of standing in front of the doctor. He held a newspaper opened in front of his face. Did he know she was there? She heard Mrs. Hall drop a glass in the kitchen, a high pitched *darn it!* The doctor put his paper down. "Oh," he said.

"You're staying here tonight, Laylah, because your grandpa died."

"He did not!" She felt her words like bullets shooting out her mouth. Her insides froze like Grandpa Johann's hand. "You're lying! I want to go over there right now. I want my momma and daddy."

"Your grandfather was very sick. You know that, don't you? He was very sick, and today he had another stroke and he died. I'm sorry. Your mother and father and your grandma are very busy tonight and need you to stay with Glenna so they can do what needs to be done. You can go there tomorrow." Then he picked up his newspaper and hid his face.

Glenna told ghost stories as they lay in bed. Then she taught Laylah the song, *The worms crawl in and the worms crawl out.* The girls argued over whether Grandpa Johann was alive or dead. Glenna insisted that her dad was not a liar. *Is. Is not. Is. Is not.* Finally Mrs. Hall called up the stairs for them to quiet down and go to sleep. Wind rattled the bedroom windows.

Laylah closed her eyes. She saw Grandpa under the ground with the worms. She shivered.

The next day after breakfast she ran to Granny's house, threw open the front door, and hurried across the living room into the bedroom where Grandpa would be saying his *Gesu, Maria, Josef,* but she was stopped by a sight so confusing it dizzied her. Grandpa's empty bed. She yelled, "Where's Grandpa?"

Granny knelt in front of her. "Grandpa died, sweetheart. You knew that." But she didn't know. She knew she was fighting something, that's what she knew. She was fighting something and had been fighting since his hand turned to ice. She knew he needed her with him and had needed her for a long time.

"Why wasn't I here?" Her tears began to stream down her face. "Grandpa wanted me with him."

Granny took her hanky from her apron pocket and wiped away her tears. "Death is no place for a little girl," she said.

A week later his ghost appeared in an ashen shadow on the bedroom ceiling. She talked to him in her mind those nights she stayed with lonely Granny Marta. "Granny misses Grandpa," Laylah's mother explained; she doesn't want to be alone when Uncle Adam goes on one of his trips. So Laylah stayed. Granny told her stories of the olden days. She wound the clocks that ticked in syncopated time. Once the lights went out, the shadow appeared and with it Grandpa's ghost repeating *Gesu, Maria, Josef.* Laylah fell asleep, lying where he once lay, his voice pulsing in her own heart's beat.

All that long winter Johann Abend's body lay in the dug-out that passed for a mausoleum in River Park Cemetery. By spring his coffin would be joined by seven more, all of which would be buried after the frost left the ground. It distracted Marta Abend all those months—his lying halfway into earth. Even though death is no place for little girls, Laylah's grandma brought it right to bed with the two of them. She snuggled close and asked impossible questions. Laylah didn't know if she was supposed to have an answer or if the questions were directed straight up, through the shadow on the ceiling and the night sky to that other world where God might live. Since she didn't know even one right thing, she held tight to Granny Marta's hand and listened as best she could.

If Grandpa wasn't altogether in the earth, Granny mumbled, might that mean his spirit like a flame would rise up, somehow, halfway out? She wondered lots of things people might not otherwise consider. How high was the water table in that land above the river? Was the bottom of the mausoleum above or below it? And how about the graves themselves? When spring arrived would her Johann be buried under water? How did caskets fare in a situation like that? Did they leak? Probably they did leak, especially those wooden ones, the only ones available since the war. They made her hands shake, those thoughts. The next day she could barely thread a needle, the way she shook. But she kept on asking, and as she asked she held Laylah's hand and squeezed as though the little girl were her only lifeline. And as she asked those questions over and over all throughout the winter, the little girl could see the water rising and could see her grandpa's open eyes looking up at her from underneath.

She could see his open mouth trying, maybe, to bring forth one more necessary word.

Laylah began believing that her grandfather was somehow still alive. Partly this intuition came from Granny's questions and partly from the shadow on Granny's ceiling. It had begun to change color, turning rusty like dry blood. Even more than both those things, though, was that Grandpa walked behind her. She felt him there. Even though he'd already disappeared when she sometimes turned quickly to catch a glimpse, she had no doubt. The very fact that she knew he'd disappeared proved that he must have been there when she felt him. Maybe it was just another of Grandpa's games. She could almost hear his laughter.

His spirit left them all in May, after the burial. For weeks she looked for him. Even the ashen stain on Grandma's ceiling now seemed empty and dull. She rode her bike out the cemetery road, past the mausoleum, which was also empty then, and on to his burial place. A mound of earth covered the top of each new grave. Grandpa's had a granite headstone that said *ABEND*, and later, when the earth settled, there would be a footstone as well with his name and the years of his life and a line from the lullaby, *Guten abend, gut nacht.* Granny Marta had explained it all to her and sung the lullaby every time she stayed the night.

In June, at the summer solstice, Laylah walked to and from the cemetery along the river rather than riding her bike on the road. The path led through a stand of tamarack under which wildflowers grew. The ground there stayed wet and little springs flowed. She crossed them with a leap or by walking a fallen log. Wild asparagus had gone to seed, all lacy at the top. She saw some moccasin flowers, yellow ones. And then she saw a fire lily burning red-orange in the afternoon shafts of light through the trees. Grandpa? But no one answered. Grandpa, she said again. Nothing. For a moment she thought she might pick the flower to place upon her grandfather's grave, but a great "not yet" rose up from her heart. She stood very still. The world spun backwards a little, like she'd come across the end of a story that really was its beginning after all. She crouched down and looked deep into the fire lily's heart. Then she leaned back against a tamarack and waited, listening as she let it be.

~ POETRY ~

The following poems are from a forthcoming collection of poems by the author titled From Grief's Deep Well.

Death of My Father

Tressi Innana Albee

From birth's
moment
fallen from
mother's careless
drunken clutch
into father's
strangling embrace.

Giant hands
held me
only
for his
own pleasure.

Golden locks
in the sea
of chestnut-haired
daughters
made me chosen.

Before words
formed on my tongue
I learned to hold
his secret touch
in silence.

My quiet torment
my steady companion.

My childhood
free-falling
the precipice
of madness,
not so much
for his
greedy caress
upon my small body,
but for
holes
left
by what
he did not do.

Every glimpse
of the father-daughter dyad
an impassioned curiosity
laced in longing.
This nagging tug
of wanting
a sense of place
in a father's
protective embrace.

Missing
a mythical other
in a primal place
of forming psyche

fracturing
shattering
splitting.

My life's path
to pick up the pieces
of myself
put them back together
even with gaps
that cannot be filled.

Poetic Sensibility

Tressi Innana Albee

Between desire
and reverie
lies ambiguity
pulsing through humanity,
made
tolerable
only through the verse
of the poet.

Do I have the courage
to answer
the poet's invitation
to meet in
the exquisite
rawness
of pure image,
in our own private
liminal between?

From dreams
to image,
to word,
poetry
captures the scent
of imagination,
the fleeting
nuanced essence
vanquished

in the presence of consciousness
becomes the ethereal clay
the poet sculpts
into language
still too inadequate
except when
wordsmithed
with devotion.

The faceless dream
voice
whispers—
pray with your ears
in numinous wonder.

Souls speak the language of poems
with the complex alphabet of dreams.

Witnessed through witnessing
crafting with awe,
while still aching with sorrow
for the delicate
encapsulation of dream
in script
where the soul
may unfurl.

Recipe for Love

Tressi Innana Albee

The first ingredient is honesty,
cupfuls of deep agonizing truth
with a sprinkling of
willingness
to risk naked vulnerability.
From honesty
Trust is born.
From Trust
Love is born.
From the birth of Love
all possibility is manifest.

Fold into the dough
of all possibility
romance and passion
vanilla scent
infusing the dough
love itself
fragranced
with tenderness.

In the heat of the fire
alchemical change ignites
primal transformation
of reciprocal connection.

Intimate embrace
Eyes locked

Upturned face
lips caress
and love
whispers
like the scent
of fresh baked bread.

High Desert Gospel

Lisa E. Baldwin

I will not live my life for a metaphor,
rather, find divinity in blackberry clouds
hung like royal birthday bunting
over the high desert. This austere Eden
desiccates and filets faith in anything
more transcendent than wind and dust,
anything more abstract than sagebrush.
Look across spare distances, and light
delivers in shimmers, like mercury loosed.
Look across to a mile-wide plank
of steel rain vanishing in the desert air.

Sound is mute, color subliminal.
Postulate life and wait: affirmation comes
from a stir in the cheat grass,
a shadow in flight, the distant rumble
of horses descending an ancient wash.

This place is mother to nothing
but time, borne out in the gnarled junipers,
witnessed in the symbiosis
of want and satisfaction as a single frame of mind.
A density of memory is the lone excess.
Petroglyphs, trail ruts, range fire chars—
recollections spanning nine-thousand years
occupy the same present and leave
still open space for a high desert miracle:
A singular sense of self,

knowing the terrible smallness of one.
It's a slow climb to a stone,
lesson of the will. Low
thunder gives it voice.

Stranded

Lisa E. Baldwin

On this outpost of sadness
fortified by long silences,
it is impossible to see clearly
a way to somewhere else,
a way out
or back or forward.
Move forward, that's what I am
supposed to do. Somehow
box up the pain, store it away
in a dark corner of my closet.
Let time then come on
to be a salve. A salvation.
But knowing the destination
is not the same
as knowing the way.

I have spent half a lifetime
looking at maps
of places I will never go,
traveling these blue abstractions alone
down remote, idyllic and exotic roads,
past edge-of-the-continent beauty,
through brilliantly engineered tunnels
of corkscrew impossibility,
old, old roads edged with fieldstone walls
curving off into some Irish mist.

Yet here, where I need it most,
there is no map
and Time is as often a Judas
as it is a Savior.
But move, I must.
Carry on, I will.
With a last look over my shoulder,
I turn my eyes toward tomorrow
and tomorrow and on
I go.

Survival: A Field Guide

Lisa E. Baldwin

I might try living like the trees,
how they go on, layering the years,
concealing the past.
Each season's accumulated woe
is tucked under, barked over.

Survival is forgetting.

"Oh no," says the dendrochronologist.
"The rings are a record,
an unforgetting. The rings
forbid forgetting. We see
springs of great growth.
The meager years show, too,
but are dominated and encircled by the more
        vigorous ones.
It is fascinating to see the whole life,
events recorded, history preserved."

An epic poem in wood.

But this is an unnatural view,
the living revealed by dying,
a life visible only in death.
On a standing tree, we see
signs of age and character,
scars like beauty marks, love knots,
wounds, embellishments.

Here and there, the sap hardens.
Forgetting is merciful.
Forgetting is a holy word.

In the high branches, hear hope disintegrating,
hear the sound of hearts breaking,
of love failing.
What is the science of betrayal?

To be cut open, bisected,
with one's life laid out on exhibit,
a brazen display of history.
This open-book record-keeping obsession
with the facts kills.
One cannot live through such exposure.
Too much history is unbearable.
Forget about it.
Dress the wounds,
layer upon layer.
Tuck under. Bark over.
Survive.

Orcas Island Revisited

Chris Bratt

Our ferry weaves through sounds of the San Juans
channeling the ancient human culture
that flourished here as indigenous nations.

I picture shoreline settlements where social rank
and status were maintained by the potlatch
ceremonial gift rituals providing an occasion for
    wealthy hosts

to share their resources with neighbors and friends
redistributing the abundant objects of value
procured by family and clans.

A civilization also known for its symbolic totems
mystical representations of animals and humans
imposing wooden carvings embracing these sacred
    kinships.

Except for a few set-aside tribal lands
trying to restore their ancestors' ways
we're left with only the mythology and museum artifacts

A people's richness consigned to oblivion
by missionaries and sickness and by another culture
that couldn't conceive of sharing the earth's wealth.

Now seaside moorage, once a haven for dugout canoes,
flaunts million-dollar cabin cruisers and yachts
communal native longhouses yielded to pricey individual
    homes.

The privileged well-heeled invaders have made
private property ownership their hallowed status symbol.
Their totems are foreboding roadside signs proclaiming:

no trespassing, private property beyond this point
no turn around, no access, no entry
dead end.

The Booty
Chris Bratt

At the edge of ocean paradise
pirates hunt for treasure
to build a driftwood bark

rigged fore and aft with junk
thrown up by the surf.
No sails or oars propel our boat
anchored in the sand,

but the child is intent on building
a place to store prizes
seized from the sea.

Unaware of potential thieves
or the extent of this spoil
she hordes hidden wealth
in her rare and precious person.

Rubies in the Mud

Diana Coogle

Walking downhill on an old logging road
pocked with the mud imprints of horses' hooves,
I was facing a blazing new year's sun
at a late morning slant,
when something—
some magic—
painted the dark shadowed side
of the deep hoofprints
a brilliant scarlet,
sickle-moon slices of blood-red earth
that disappeared in the shadows
as I walked
and reappeared in the sun,
dazzlingly bright,
deeply red.
And all the little rocks
with their backs to the sun
lying in the muddy road
turned red, too—
as deep as jewels.
The road was suddenly studded
with the riches of the mines of Mogok,
the rubies of Burma.
King Thebaw, Tharawadi,
Anne of Brittany, Rosser Reeves, and Alan Caplan
can wear their Mogok rubies in their crowns
and on their fingers.
They cannot be wealthier than I
with my hundreds of rubies in the mud.

Swimming with Manatees

Diana Coogle

Camping on the Manatee River in central Florida
when my son was a baby
and his father and I on our way to Jamaica
(for some crazy hippy reason),
I swam in water tea-brown with tannic acid
but clear and clean.
I swam every day
between nursing my baby
making camp meals
writing in my journal
and studying the Tarot.
It was a thrill to think I was swimming with manatees,
huge mammals of the water world
working their prehensile lips over river vegetation
under my dangling legs.

On one moonless midnight I thought
for some crazy hippy reason
how exciting it would be to swim
in the dark river under the dark sky
as though swimming through midnight itself.
So I slipped from the tent,
leaving my baby and his father asleep,
walked the path to the river's shore,
and slipped naked into the river.

It was indeed exciting to swim
through the moonless black sky and the black waters

with manatees swimming silently below me
until I thought
of alligators
who would not know the difference
between my legs dangling in the dark water
and any other piece of meat and might
for some crazy hippy reason
try a bite.

The thought gave pause
but not much pause
before I swam to shore,
leaving all creatures in the Manatee River
to swim in the dark
without me.

It's a Woman's War

Dolores Durando

A baby on her hip, another in her belly,
Misery was her only friend, and life was just a lie.
She plodded on, nor looked behind,
And prayed that she could die.

The barren ground was cold and gray,
Her spirit was the same,
It mattered not who's right or wrong
Or where to place the blame.

All hope had fled, but hunger stayed
Beside her like a friend.
A desolate, pitiless, unforgiving land
Promised death to those who strayed.

She prayed for death, with every step,
Her burden was too great.
No other way to leave this land,
This land of kill and hate.

Her hungry child held tight her skirt,
Starvation slowed her pace.
No laughing, chubby baby, this,
But death with a baby's face.

The baby faltered, and now he fell,
His mother knelt beside him,
Held his body close, and prayed

As the other stirred within.
Death hurried then, and held them fast,
His lover's arms encircled.
He promised peace in paradise
And they were warm at last.

Requiem for a Tired Old Car

Dolores Durando

The front tires have gone flat.
The carburetor's plugged.
They say the oil pan leaks.
Wipers don't work, the windshield's bugged.
The key—where in hell is it at?

It's low on oil, I doubt there's much gas.
The meter doesn't work, I'm sure.
I'd be out on the highway hiking my ass.
How long can my poor feet endure?

The clutch has gone out; that gives me no thrill.
The upholstery for sure is shot.
The old car stalls—possibly will
start one more time, but maybe not.

I'll roll into heaven, riding the rims.
There's a go in the old girl yet.
But the sun goes down and the headlights dim.
The angels sing, "Don't touch the car
the paint's still wet,
and she's come so very far."

Wish I Hadn't Died

Dolores Durando

We've grown old and sit by the fire
remembering days gone by.
I remember it, as it was, and tell it true,
but she's such a terrible liar!

Now the fire has turned to ashes and I've sent her on ahead
to check at the Gate for our chances.
Will she go to my heaven, or I to hers?
Or are they one and the same?
Can St. Peter withstand her loving advances?
Let's pray he's on top of his game!

"Halo?" she puzzles, "Wings, feathers, too?
Is there a bird in residence here?"
She drools a bit, then sharpens her claws,
and there goes our salvation, I fear.

But she sweet-talks the Gateman and shimmies inside,
and I'm on the outside, begging in.
She blows me a kiss, her position secure,
and indicts me for the original sin.

In my heart I have lusted,
and now I've been busted.
I wish I hadn't died.

After Stafford

Anna Elkins

Ask me what the snow holds.

Ask me the shape of my own hands
    as I've held the promise of spring.

I have chosen to live with winter
    in the naked trees.

Ask me how these trees hold still enough
    to live, and I will climb them.

See that lowest branch? It could carry
    the weight of childhood
    a tropical continent
    a sister and brother
        playing seven-hand Rummy.

Ask me what the sky sheds—
    rain, days, maybes.

Maybe we fall like snow,

    or maybe we fly.

Equinox
Beate Foit

Thirty-five years ago today
was our first "official" date.

We drove to a reservoir
in the Eifel mountains
the woods surrounding it
were brilliant in their fall hues.

Your "Steve McQueen" smile
dazzled me,
you impressed me
because you listened.

You cared—
reminding me of my injured back
while I climbed on trees and
balanced on rocks.

But I didn't feel pain—
being with you
I only felt carefree, light, and exhilarated
that first day of autumn.

Your eyes kept mine hostage
I lost myself in them
trusting you
with my heart.

Not only the season was changing
but my life as well
turning a new leaf
in the book of my life.

The painful divorce
a thing of the past,
and life with you
just beginning.

There Is a Story

Beate Foit

There is a story hidden in each day
unfolding without our contribution

Sun rays made visible by the cold air
fall on frozen ground
softening it slowly as the day progresses.

Steaming breath like a billowing cloud
dances around the faces of creatures
hiding in the shadows

No need to know the ending of the story
or its beginning

we are in the story—mere puppets
placed where we live by providence
living in a place predestined long ago

ever moving, never resting
secrets are unfolding as the journey continues

comfort comes from knowing
that a continuum exists
which—pulled by invisible forces—
moves and guides us
on our incredible journey through life.

Strangest Things

Carol Hoon

The strangest things still make me cry:
Falling-down barns and the wood piling up,
A yellow lab riding in the back of an old pickup truck,
A rainbow against a dove grey sky, with no wires in the
    way.

But, you don't see the things I see and you never felt the way
I feel. Six long months go crawling by, now snow flies, there
are no more rainbows in the sky, but still the strangest things
can make me cry.

Coffee beans on the fair trade aisle, only once did make
    you smile, but once was not enough for me.
A sad, sad song on the radio; Amos and Todd and Patty
    are all crying over you, too.
A chocolate chip cookie in the middle of summer, with no
    fear of calories.

I'm leaving California on the yellow brick road, but I'm
walking down the road with the wrong hand in mine because
you don't see the things I see and you never felt the way I feel.
Six long months go crawling by, snow flies, no more rainbows
in the sky, and still the thought of you just makes me cry.

A Lament
Seth Kaplan

I hear the voice
Sounding like the ancients
Sounding like a wish
Calling, calling
Am I doing enough?
It resonates & engulfs & pierces
Am I doing enough?
And even the fullness of this sky cannot hold my tears
as my child's heart opens and the sadness rushes in

I remember, no, I never forget
Finding that one dead bird, alone
on the stripped land of a future apartment building
Knowing no one would grieve for her
was too much for my child's heart to bear
And I held ceremony, gathered twigs for cover
Offered prayer to honor her shortened life
And I grieved anew as my family laughed how cute
Over dinner later 'round our shared table in our
        suburban home

I remember, no, I never forget
My band of brothers discovering the Ladybug Hotel
Amidst the forbidden acreage of a future housing tract
Knowing, even then, the massacre to come from the army
        of caterpillar tractors
Like suburban terrorists, we gathered in the shadows
        after dinner

Removing the signs and markers of civilization
In the vain hope that the occupiers would lose their way
And the inevitability of destruction was too much for my
    child's heart to bear
As I witnessed thousands of ladybugs crushed by the
    wheels of progress
And this time I told no one when I cried amidst the
    erected skeletons of development

Through the decades, I open my child's heart to these
    fundamental moments
And I lament
Oh, God, am I doing enough?
When I bring out my child's heart
I feel the pain of every living thing
And every thing is living
There is always someone dying alone
Always families and communities distressed
I grieve for every child given less than a chance
I grieve for every individual demonized for being
    different
I grieve for the poets & dreamers & prophets
who live on our streets and outside their minds
I grieve for the wolf who is killed for being a wolf
I grieve for mother earth who is unloved
by her most ambitious children

And I have tried, dear God, I have tried
To become powerful enough
To be eloquent enough
To be brave enough

To be wise enough
To keep my child's heart open enough
To use my grief as a compass
To do what I can
To know I have done enough
But it never is, it never is
Enough

I long to embrace the caress of sleep
And I cry today
Because I am tired, so tired
And I know I've been tired before
And I haven't done enough
And I can't hold anymore
And I need to be held

Turning 60

Seth Kaplan

Words escape me
I drop bread crumbs
To find my way back to misplaced thoughts
I leave food scraps
As offerings to Raven
I gaze into the silvering dawn
Longing for a glimpse of ebony wings
A reminder of the wind dance
There is something I want to say
It will come to me

And so I am 60
And what does it mean
That so many are surprised and always, wow,
60, you don't look it
And so I am 60
Even less time
Than I am from Oregon

What do I know of 60
And those of the 60 clan
Say it is great, you will love it
And those of this land
Say it is great, you will love it
And what do they know
Of a lifetime, no a lineage, of worry
That informs this moment, my place in this place

With age comes wisdom
With wisdom comes humility,
Sitting on one shoulder,
Wonder on the other
I was once a super hero, and now
I look out at this valley
Shaped by time

White Wonder

Linda Kappen

White wonder out of the sky
Dancing through tree limbs and branches so high
Each falling separately but at the same speed
A downward fall twisting, rocking, spiraling
Some straight and some free
Different sizes and shapes as they move to the ground
Where they gather as one
A blanket so sound

Your Eyes Paint the Canvas

Linda Kappen

Your eyes paint the canvas
Through your photographic lens
Touching the world beyond us
Laying light in every crevice from within.

Shadows fall and lead you to another place afar
Sanctify your presence
Fairies dance around your heart.

Natural world pulls you
A magnet to your soul
Let your gifts guide you
Love what they behold

For the Children

Joy La Spina

In their faces Light reflected, Love begotten, Life Anew...
Ancient Souls, they've come to lead us, if we'll only see
    them through...
For the children let us smile, let us know ourselves as free;
Let us wrap our arms around them; giving Love is how
    we'll see,
The truth our children bring to us, God's gift beyond the
    Sun,
Master teachers in small bodies, Blessed angels
    everyone...

In their eyes is Light reflected, Love begotten, Life Anew
Ancient Souls, they've come to teach us, if we'll only
    know it's true...
For the children come to be our hope, a sacred prayer
    conceived.
The wisdom which they share is real. They need to be
    believed...

Oh let us listen for the children, let us hear beyond the
    tears.
Can we really be there for them and sacrifice our fears?
To be with them in our highest love, our highest hopes
    and dreams,
Remembering our gentleness as simple as it seems...
For the children—celebrate in Peace. Sing and dance
    and show you care...
It's only You, your deepest self they really want to share.

So bless the little children as they travel here with you,
In their hearts Light is reflected, Love begotten, Life
   renewed.

Heart Flood '05

Joy La Spina

The long rain coming
Day after day
Streaming, soaking
Now week after week
Only brief glimpses of light
Patches of blue, one rainbow
Creeks turn to rivers
Everywhere wet
Leaks, puddles, floods
Drenched soggy earth
The forest is dripping

Sitting to listen
Edges of body mind blur
Its waters merging
With emotion, tears and rain
All rushing the same

Moving me inward, hushed softness
A place that shines, space between storms
Prayers pour through
To open like the sky
Offering
And be thankful for this
Generous watering of life
My deepening heart

under an applegate point

Ty Thomas Luckman

Old Madrone falls dead on the ground next to poison oak
    & spider webs
of Manzanita. The upward path breaks slightly to the right,
    then abruptly
swings left as it ascends higher. The vineyard below cuts
    into numbered
segments of sevens, hedged by the property line of tall
    grass and the
Applegate River. The rusted, steel gate at the top of the
    ridge still
holds; weather and teenage carvings of love incapable of
    pulling it to
the ground. Bolted brown chain links fix to the side of
    sunken posts—
secured and steady for decades to come. The wild lilac at
    the top of the
point outstretches its arms to the west, accusing the sun of
    loving
warmth and unforgiving sustenance. A rouged apple tree
    withers against
the setting of the triple mountain cake. Our star falls as
    the planet rotates.

A Stylish Folk
Alice Gelston Migliore

They lie in glass cases
Dried corpses
From the Takla Makan Desert.
One Thousand B.C.
They rest exposed and naked
With bits of woven garments
To cover their shrunken privates.

Around them, in glass cases,
Are displayed the lives they led,
Leather boots they sewed,
Cloth they wove,
Clay pots they used,
And woven hats in all shapes and sizes,
For remember, they too were a stylish folk,
three thousand years ago.

But now they lie, without eyes,
Lipless mouths of yellow teeth.
They weave no more.
They dance no more.
They have become the dried, shrunken leather
And frayed, torn cloth
They spent their lives creating.

One has been named "Sleeping Beauty."
Black, shrunken, hairless.
She waits for three thousand years,

But no kiss from lips moist and young,
Could ever bring her back to life.

Some say that, early in the morning,
Before the museum opens its doors,
One can hear the faint sound of frolic,
As they play the old drums,
The old pipes, and the old strings,
And dance about their glass cases
Wearing nothing but woven hats in all shapes and sizes.

For remember, they too were a stylish folk,
three thousand years ago.

Gourmet Coffee

Alice Gelston Migliore

He placed a bag of coffee on the counter,
Some Moroccan-Arabic blend—"Foglifter."
It was the tired hour, and I was thinking
A cup would taste so good.
He wore an old denim jacket with the sheepskin collar
That didn't go with the gourmet coffee at 14.99 a pound.
Old scuffed cowboy boots, worn jeans, an unkempt beard,
I sized him up as one of those old guys
Who lives on a mining claim out in the Applegate.

But then he spoke to the clerk in a pleasing voice,
East Coast maybe, definitely educated,
And I looked into his face, and his tired blue eyes met
      mine,
And he included me in his comments.

Big snow coming tonight, he said.
I'm gonna go home and grind up this stuff,
And make a big pot of nice, hot coffee.
Then I'm gonna sit and drink the whole damned thing
And watch the snow come down.
Sounds great, Jack, said the clerk
As she counted out his change into his big wrinkled hand.
She waited while he stuffed the bills and coins into his
      pocket,
Picked up the bag, nodded his head,
And turned to leave the store.

I watched through the window as he walked out to his
    rusty old rig,
And I had the strangest notion.
Why not run alongside, take his arm,
And join him for a cup of that gourmet coffee.
I'd had a bad day myself,
And I could use a cup of Foglifter.
But instead, I paid for the trail mix
And drove off in my own rusty rig.

Two days later, same store, same tired hour, new bag of
    trail mix,
Same life, same undercurrent of sadness,
But a different man at the counter before me,
Buying a can of shaving cream,
And a loaf of twelve-grain bread.

Hear about Jack? he asked the clerk. Jack Miller?
No, she said, not looking up from the register.
What about Jack Miller?
Blew his brains out a day or two ago,
The night of that big storm, I think it was.

Doesn't surprise me, she said,
As she counted the change out into his smooth, soft hand.

Then she picked up my bag of trail mix and stared at it
    thoughtfully.
The night of the storm. He was in here that night.
That's right. He was buying… she paused, he was
    buying…

I finished her thought.
Moroccan-Arabic coffee, I said. Foglifter, 14.99 a pound.

You're right, she said, Foglifter, 14.99 a pound.
That man sure loved his gourmet coffee.

Foglifter, I thought, as I walked out of the store.
I guess it didn't work, or maybe it did.

Remembering Bobby

Alice Gelston Migliore

An old friend calls with the news from home.
Bobby Scott was killed in a car wreck.

Pleased to have something to report
From a place where nothing much happens,
My friend gives all the details of the crash.

It happened while Bobby was driving to work.
He reached over to take a swig from a coffee cup,
Or, more likely, from a can of beer, she added.
The car went off the road and hit a tree.
His neck was broken,
And the steering wheel crushed his heart.
He wasn't wearing a seat belt.

"You remember him, don't you?
He was about our age,
Give or take a year or two."

A scene, lost for decades in my memory,
Suddenly comes into focus.

Bobby Scott had changed overnight from a chubby imp,
Friend Sally's pesky little brother,
Into a tall, gaunt teenager
With a shock of blond hair falling over one blue eye.
We were gathered in his mother's sewing room
At the back of the house.

Table, ironing board and clothes rack
Pushed against the wall
To create a dance floor.
We were teaching Bobby how to jitterbug,
A prerequisite for popularity in high school.

As Bobby danced alone, smoothly and rhythmically
On the shiny, smooth linoleum floor
To the strains of The Battle of New Orleans,
We elders looked on with approval.
Bobby was cute; he was a good dancer;
He was going to be popular in high school.

I moved away and heard news of old friends
Through infrequent calls from home.
Bobby married young, had two children, and divorced.
With the help of hard liquor and friendly beers,
He grew old before his time.
On my rare visits home, he would be pointed out to me,
A disheveled, bearded man with a dog and a gun.

"He turned out to be nothing but an old drunk,"
My friend added.

But my kind memory could not accept such an epitaph.
I shut my eyes and began to hum The Battle of New Orleans,
And Bobby Scott appeared, dancing around the room,
Sliding his feet and snapping his fingers,
Frozen at the peak of his potential.
He was cute; he was a good dancer;
And he was going to be popular in high school.

Markings

H. Ní Aódagaín

I am marked.

In these first months of loving,
the ecstatic, fiery force
scorching through us
leaves signs on my body.

On the surface
they are accidents

I trip on the rug
the iron touches
    my bare thigh
your tooth catches
    my lip

A bruise,
    a burn,
        a blister

           appears

and I am marked.

What does it mean?
That we are joined
so deeply
you have entered me
so completely

My body, like a mirror
brandishes
the places of union

Lip,
   thigh,
      knee

points of contact
moments of fusion

I am marked,

our love
the tattooist's pen

Summer Days

H. Ní Aódagaín

Summer days link together like a bracelet
each bead a beauty,
as sun rises soft against the mountains
birds knock on wood to make home
the old dog, dear companion, stretches and yawns,
deciding to live, yet once more, this new day
at our side.

The blazing, brutal heat of July, the hottest
on record in this southern Oregon town,
has abated

and for the first time in too long,
evening alights softly
on our shoulders.

A fresh breeze, cool and casual,
like the perfect summer shawl
gently strokes our open arms

grateful and giddy
we welcome her
this rare visitor into our midst.

Tomorrow may bring the return
of a sun so scalding,
we fear the end of the world

apocalyptic prophecies recited,
half in jest,
half in wonderment

the rivers' waters, not enough
to keep the earth and all its inhabitants
sated and safe from the raging fire.

But, today, the air
murmurs a sweet song,
the grapes grow plump,
golden green goblets
of nectar on my tongue

the first leaves of autumn
float silently down
to lie upon the dying grass

and I bow to the magnificent mystery of it all.

Chat

Joan Peterson

Through the pat-pat
drops on the roof
comes another sound:
gold coins thrown
to the wind. Chimes glitter
against the moon, rattles

and whistles thrust out
on fields of grain.
All night notes drift
past our window filling
our dreams. By day

we sing back, tunes planted
in our minds. A yellow-breasted chat
returns our attempts at mimicry.
In lives so separate here
we all sing the same song.
We grunt and caw, a little off key.

The chat responds with bird-call
wisdom. He gets our attention,
a "look-here" phrase,
then sings lazy notes to
bring the dog home. Sometimes
it's the sound of a dirge:

one heart beating in the center
of the earth.

Jay
Joan Peterson

Drone of the forest
Clone of your species
Jackhammer
Backhoe
Egg robber
Jay

You weave your way
around bird feeders
rowing wing beats
crowding out junco,
creeper, siskin and finch.

Shek shek shek:
harsh vocabulary
for the prideful
philanderer.
We know your tricks.

Hurry up, fall. Cool
our season enough
to freeze this short-tailed
blue-shield armored greed.
His stellar performance
is blocking my view.

Swallowtail

Joan Peterson

Stained glass wings
yellow and black
spread out along the lilac
slow motion flutter,
suddenly airborne
surfing the wind.

Resembling japonica
my red visor hat
at the proper tilt,
I become an airstrip
for landing.

Yellow and black
twittering wings
send messages
vibrant with sound.

I say it's a sign
when a butterfly
chooses your self
as the place to pause
and meditate.

You become
a flower.

Will You Sleep with My Husband?
Jane Robin

When women ask, "Will you sleep with my husband?"
It used to mean:

Will you join us in a wild night of dancing and drinking
and running around town in a sexually charged little pack
knowing we would come home to set the sheets flailing
while we all laugh and
enjoy the company.

Or it meant:

Can you teach him something because
I don't know how to ask
for this (whisper, whisper).
The secret thing she longs for.

Now, in our age it means:

I'm dying.
Would you be the one
to comfort him while
he weeps?
I am chained to this dialysis machine, and
our life has become so grim.

I want him to find moments of
happiness, to see that fresh ease

on his face that I knew so well when we first
fell in love.

Go with him to hear his band play,
sit at the poker table and play your hand.
Attend the poet laureate reading and
walk home discussing some miraculous
phrase that made your hearts soar.

Will you sleep with my husband? now means:

Will you be there?
Will you accept this half-partnered life? Can I trust you
with this sacred love
that has limped the distance?

The "Pond"

Christina Strelova

Chirpings of frogs
Loud
In the forest?
No. In the field.
Like glazed porcelain,
green and brown;
In the drainage ditch.

They sing songs of love.
Yearning...in the rain.

Soon, tadpoles
Thousands it seems.
Such joy!
I bring fish food.
They hose the flakes
Into their tiny mouths.

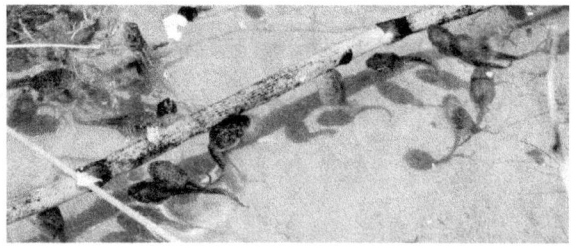

Warm spring days have come;
Only small puddles remain.
Many have died.

I make dams.
Filling small reservoirs
With well water from the hose.

One day, I forget,
And leave the hose running.
Water has spilled over the dams
And tadpoles have followed.
I spend hours returning them to their "pond."
I put in a drain for overflow.

Dragonflies and small wasps arrive.
Water beetles join the pollywogs.
Tiny buds of rear legs are forming.
I bring plants from the bullfrog pond.
The tads are ecstatic.

Fish food lands on the water.
The tadpoles surface, turning on their backs
To expose their iridescent bronze and white bellies,
And vacuum the flakes with their huge mouths.

These creatures are clean and efficient.
Those who are weak or who perish are consumed.
All that is edible is consumed.
So that they may grow and transform.

Rear legs grow larger.
They are dragged along,
Pushed, by the enormous tail.
The tail diminishes as the legs grow.

The rear legs become a new powerful engine.
Front legs are budding.

There is a yearning, for air.
On the water's edge,
The primeval movement onto the land begins.

I see minuscule but perfectly formed froglings
Popping along the banks of the "ponds."
Joyously trying out these new bodies.
Searching for bugs in the weeds.
Serious joy!

Summer has come.

The frogs have moved into the grass.
The water beetles are moving on, too;
They are replaced by snails and algae.
The pond becomes a wetland
Soon to transform
Into an impression in the field
Waiting for the rains.

Alders to Alders

Barbara Summerhawk

I was trying to dig my heels into the
sands of time
when I tripped and fell
back into the aches and pains of
Being.
Before I was a Leo I was a
Brownie; both IDs chosen by
Someone Other,
not me, never graduating to a
Virgo, say, or a Girl Scout.
I hang around on Humbug hillsides
in love with the Milky Way.
My elder alder, too, tripped and fell,
crossed the creek,
creating a hardwood bridge to and from
new possibilities for metaphor.
Without that giant, mossy giver of shade,
the steelhead packed up, moved downstream,
Humbug Creek too hot to handle here,
now open, more Milky Way to see.
My companion for nearly thirty years
shady, sighing,
part and parcel of my main stem,
will now warm winter friends.

Ashes to ashes,
Alders to alders,
We await our seedling renewal.

Maiden, Woman, Crone...

Barbara Summerhawk

I'm up the trail here
Looking back and
Stretching out my hand across the strata
Separating our ages.
I'm here
Lifting you up,
The you that was me.
Come, I have some secrets to tell you
How to thread the needle that can
Sew up the gap in our lives.
You are so young and cynical and
So empty of nice things to say about
Yourself.
You try to, but don't believe; I do.
I'm here
To help you cross the
Minefield of maturity.
Somewhere up ahead I know
There's another me smiling, reaching out her hand
Linking all of us, all the "me"s
Inside
Waiting to tell us about all
The new forms we'll take,
The new ways we'll create
Together with
Nothing more to prove.
She is whispering a word
I whisper to you,
Come.

Humbug Perspective

Paul Tipton

A few things have changed in forty years,
Up past the forks of Humbug, and below.
Only a few of the real old-timers left
Most others passed or moved to town.
Lots of us 70s back-to-the-landers
Have tucked away the long hair, beards and tie-dye
Yet retain our sense of community connection
Enriched by years of potlucks and work parties,
Shared child care and camping trips together.
It's an aspect of life we're happy not to have missed.
These days the early sunrise from grow lights
And the roar of fans ventilating greenhouses
Alter the peace and quiet so cherished here.
Tall fences spread like viruses along property lines
Doing little to hide what's happening behind.
Cars of workers and buyers leave long dust plumes
Speeding up the once quiet gravel roads.
Many who wished to grow and smoke a little
Way back when, never expected the onslaught
That recent years have brought to the creek.
One thing has stayed the same: they say
Humbug still produces the best bud around.
One can only hope they'll also grow to know
The golden rule of neighborliness.

Alone Together

Stew Towle

Sometimes child's pose
   is my holding-back-the-tears face,
   in a house full of friends,
   when my body feels like the end piece
   of the burnt loaf
   in our big batch of garlic bread;
   when I wish I could make you laugh.
The folding of the body
   that makes this alone I feel a little
   warmer, a little more
   useful.

                            Flexibility and weight
                        loss, memory and craving.
Sometimes every experience reminds me
   of a love I couldn't keep;
   that Karma is a game with countless rounds.
Sometimes all my meditation feels like
   a fancy way of complaining, to someone else
   who doesn't care.

Some mornings, as my land-mates cough
   and fill the coffeepot,
   I feel like I'm still sitting at the edge
   of the playground, waiting for one
   of the other children to invite me
   to play.

Buff

Thalia Truesdell

Awakened by a sudden gust of wind
lacy treetops rattle a death dance
sending crackling leaves cascading,
twirling, swirling upon the parched earth,
dried grasses and cockleburs,
so much crumbling tinder.

Struggling powerfully to penetrate
the thick smoke of wildfires
the weakened sun casts a faint
golden glow upon the thirsty earth,
sucking the very chlorophyll
from the last of the hillside grasses.

Cicadas settle into an incessant trill
when the wind dies down,
punctuated by periods of eerie silence,
the oppressive air swallowing birdsong,
and this buff-colored landscape
lolls languidly through a hot summer afternoon.

Musings on a Table Rock

Marina Walker (Photo by Park Walker)

As I hike up the steep incline
I am aware of descending back in time
each step marking a span
of geologic proportions.
A signboard tells me how once long ago
high above where I stand
a river etched its way
through a vast flow of molten rock.

When at last I reach the top
I emerge into a different world.
I feel suspended in time and space,
encircled by mountains
and uplifted, as if on a plate,
to the vastness of the sky.
Around me an array of greens and yellows
clothe the table-like expanse.

In the distance, vernal pools are shimmering
casting a magic spell.
They are teeming with life on this springy day
I kneel to inspect the frolic.
Then, as I pass by
the pools assume a mirror-like stance
I am surprised by the reflection of Mt. McLoughlin
upended in a pool.

Old tracks from aircraft
form a linear highway across the plateau
leading me to the southern rim.
Hearing a hum and feeling a vibration
emerging from the valley below,
I am shaken from my dream-like suspension.
In the distance, toy-like cars and trucks ply their way
through a terrain of miniature dimensions.

I find a place to rest
on the hard and rough andesitic rim.
It occurs to me that the River
might once have flowed at my feet.
Turkey vultures are perched nearby.
Ungainly and unappealing at rest,
I am awed by their grace as they soar
in an exquisite dance with thermals.

Below me the roguish River belies its strength
gently snaking its way through a collage
of ranches, orchards and gravel mines.
I reflect on water's incessant need to flow,

carving its way and washing silty residues out to sea.
I marvel at this monument, upon which I now sit,
a testament to the River's persistent, fluid labor
and to the passage of time.

The Elizabeth Poems

Christin Lore Weber

The following three poems were written upon the death of the author's sister after a ten-year struggle with breast cancer.

A Branch

Broken but not detached
Hangs splintered
Bark split open to the heartwood
Twisted, tangled,
Blood colored from the wind
Sheering through.

I don't know what to do.

It's nothing, she tells me,
Her face streaked crimson,
Her feet, her hands, her neck and chest
Above her scars
All aflame.

We.
Will.
Not.
Remember.
Why.

A Box

From underneath her stairs,
Sits open on the cluttered parlor floor.
Newsprint blackens her hands.

It flakes as she unwraps the old
Treasures once fine enough to keep
Through generations.

A baptismal dress of dragonfly wings
And torn lace. She left it
In the box too long.

"Even a museum wouldn't want this anymore."
She fingers an iron-colored water stain
We both know can never be removed.

The stain matches perfectly the tuft of hair
Remaining on her head. She lifts her hand
To touch a chemo-rash that floods her face.

"I used to love my house."
She reaches for me to help her rise.
"I hate it now."

Lilacs

Torn off the tree
Clutter her kitchen shelf.
I cannot watch them fall.

I am haunted by a scent—
The churchyard by the river
On her wedding day.

Rain in lilac clusters.

Why did she snap the branch
Step into the current
But didn't tip her head
To drink?

Infinite Life
Greeley Wells

I didn't think of this then
    I think of it now
youth then
    innocence and energy
age now and perspective
    great amounts of time and experience
even so little as life is
    infinite time and meaning

Moon Sun Dance

Greeley Wells

The moon does a monthly orbit around the earth
The earth a yearly one around the sun
When the sun is low in winter
The full moon is high
The sun is high
All the warmth of summer
While the full moons dip low to the horizon
The smaller chards of moon visit each month in opposites
Lower and lower in winter
Higher and higher in summer
This dance this play of the solar system
Echoes bigger cosmic plays and dances
That all tickle the mind
And delight

Tree Rain

Greeley Wells

At the southern end

    of the Redwoods

high in a mountain forest

    a thick marine layer fills the sky with cloud mist

condensing on each minuscule needle

    dry all around

and complete silence

    but for a steady rain within the drip line

~ AUTHOR BIOGRAPHIES ~

Tressi Innana Albee began writing in journals at the age of twelve and has kept a journal ever since. She was published in the 2012 and 2013 Annual Literary Review of Pacifica Graduate Institute. In 2014, Tressi published her master's thesis, *Archetypes of the Womb: As Revealed Through the Sisterhood of Sarah and Hagar*. She lives with her family in southern Oregon, where she has a private practice of psychotherapy and is studying for her PhD in depth psychology.

Lisa E. Baldwin is a teacher and writer who believes poetry is necessary for a good life. A fifth-generation Oregon native, she draws on the beauty, diversity, and history of our place in her poetry. She lives on a little farm in the Lower Applegate Valley with her husband and honeybees.

Gay Bradshaw, who holds doctorate degrees in ecology and psychology, is the author of *Elephants on the Edge: What Animals Teach Us about Humanity,* an award-winning book that explores the minds, emotions, and lives of elephants. Her work established the field of trans-species psychology and includes her founding of the Kerulos Center in order to "bring science and sanctuary together in service to all animals." Gay and her family have lived in the Applegate since 1955. Her website is www.kerulos.org, and her email address is bradshaw@kerulos.org.

Chris Bratt was born and raised in San Francisco, earned a BA in industrial arts from San Francisco State University, and is a lifetime member of the United Brotherhood of Carpenters and Joiners of America. He has taught carpentry and industrial arts. Upon moving to Applegate in 1976, Chris worked as a building contractor while managing his family's woodland farm. He is a founding board member of the Applegate Partnership and Watershed Council, the Geos Institute, and other environmental groups. His email address is xopher5317@gmail.com.

A Georgia native, **Diana Coogle** graduated magna cum laude from Vanderbilt, studied at Harvard, and was a Marshall Scholar, a Woodrow Wilson Teaching Fellow, and a finalist in the Oregon Book Awards and in a national playwriting contest. Diana has taught at the University of Oregon, Rogue Community College, and Gothenburg University, Sweden. In 2012 she earned a PhD in Old English. For 40 years she lived without electricity on an Applegate mountainside. She now lives there with electricity. Diana's email address is dicoog@gmail.com. She blogs at dianacoogle.blogspot.com.

Dolores Durando, author of *And Yesterday is Gone, Beyond the Bougainvillea,* and *Out of the Darkness*, has served on mental health advisory boards and spent fourteen years as a board member of *Asset*, a national magazine, for which she wrote short stories. She retired at seventy and moved to Oregon, where she has been writing, painting, and sculpting. She lives independently in a cottage on the doorstep of Grayback Mountain with her corgi and two cats.

Laurie Easter holds an MFA in writing from Vermont College of Fine Arts and is a creative nonfiction editor for its journal for the arts. Among her literary honors are a nomination for a Pushcart Prize, a fellowship from the Vermont Studio Center, and a "Notable Essay" listing in *Best American Essays 2015* for her essay "Crack My Heart Wide Open." She lives in a funky little cabin "off the grid" with her family and a menagerie of animals. Laurie's website is www.laurieeaster.com.

Anna Elkins is a traveling poet and painter. Anna earned a BA in art and English and an MFA and Fulbright Fellowship in poetry. She has written, painted, and taught on six continents. Her art hangs on walls around the world, and she has published four books, most recently the illustrated "children's book for grownups," *And: The Story of More*. Anna has set up her easel and writing desk in the mythical State of Jefferson. Her website address is www.annaelkins.com, and her email address is ae@annaelkins.com.

Beate Foit, originally from Germany, moved to Williams from Santa Cruz, California, eleven years ago. Beate has been writing for over twenty years, primarily for her own enjoyment. A translator by profession since 1984, she has written search cues for an online forum and published poems in online publications. She is a member of the Applegate Poets and is working on publishing a children's book. Beate enjoys language in all the forms of books, plays, and songs. Her email address is beatefoit@gmail.com.

Connie Fowler says she figures she ought to be considered an "old-timer" because for forty-two years she has called the Little Applegate River and, specifically, Buncom her home, where she and her husband, Ben, raised quarter horses and commercial cattle. She has written for various publications and was co-author of a book about Buncom. She enjoys riding her horse, gardening, singing, song writing, and writing.

Carol Hoon has been loving life with her family in the Siskiyou mountains of the Applegate for five years. She is a mathematician and former rocket scientist who gave up her left-brained career to raise her children and live in harmony with the rhythm of the seasons. She published her first book, *Cookies for Christmas: Recipes and Memories from my Mother*, in early 2015. Contact Carol through her email address at orcarolhoon@gmail.com.

Morgan Jordan lives in the Applegate Valley with her husband, Jack, in the company of one hunter cat, a blue-eyed dog, and one Gizmo. She has been a performer and musician for over thirty years and has published short stories in magazines such as the *Copperfield Review, Timeless Tales, Midnight Circus* and online in *Fiction Magazine*'s Romance volume. Her novella, *Wind in My Sails*, is available at Amazon. Morgan's email address is 3608books@gmail.com.

Lily Myers Kaplan is author of *Two Rare Birds: A Legacy of Love*, a book about her brother's and sister's years with terminal cancer. She is the founder of SoulWorks and the Spirit of Resh Foundation, which seeks to build awareness that facing death is about choosing how to live. An ordained minister and life coach for nearly thirty years, Lily uses story as a form of healing with individuals, couples, and groups. See more about her at www.aboutsoulworks.com and www.reshfoundation.org. Her email address is aboutsoulworks@gmail.com.

Seth Kaplan is a recent immigrant from the Bay Area. He lives in the Applegate with his wife, Lily, and his dog, Shayna. After decades building livable communities through strategic partnerships, he seeks to find that which he has created. In his work, he is committed to helping people who are doing good in the world to do even better. Seth's website is www.sethkaplanconsulting.com, and his email address is sethkap55@gmail.com.

Linda Kappen grew up exploring the banks and woods of the Rogue River west of Grants Pass. She has lived in the Applegate with her husband since 1980. Working with children and parents through her job and volunteer work at Applegate School is, for her, a rewarding experience. She has a Naturalist Certificate through Siskiyou Field Institute and is especially interested in the butterflies and moths of southern Oregon. Writing poetry is a favorite pastime. Linda's email address is humbugkapps@hotmail.com, and she maintains a Facebook page called "Butterflies and Moths of the Pacific Northwest."

Joy La Spina feels she has been "lucky enough to live in beautiful Williams, Oregon, for twenty-five years, to have a wonderful partner, and to enjoy an abundance of wonderful children, grandchildren, and friends." Currently, her work is in eldercare, and she still provides a bit of massage therapy. She has loved poetry and nature for as long as she can remember.

Ty Thomas Luckman was born and raised in Grants Pass, Oregon. He obtained a BS in social science-criminology from Southern Oregon University and is a writer of short stories, poetry, and comic books. Ty's email address is luckmanty@yahoo.com.

Haley Morgan May is a Licensed Massage Therapist who graduated from the Ashland Institute of Massage in June, 2009. Originally from Wyoming, she earned a BA in English at Southern Oregon University, then moved to the Applegate. With a passion for personal growth and learning, she has traveled to Mexico, Hawaii, Fiji, New Zealand, and across the United States. She divides her time between massage, gardening, writing, and working at her grandparents' forest farm in the Applegate. Haley's email address is hmaylmt@gmail.com.

Kayleigh B. McKey was born and raised in Medford but moved to the Applegate in 2012, where she lives on a dairy farm. She graduated from Hidden Valley High School in 2015 and is looking forward to a quiet life writing and working in a small, local occupation. Her favorite music is classic rock, her favorite book genre historical fiction. She dreams of settling in Ireland with her own library and farm and a man she can grow old with.

Alice Gelston Migliore has a BA in creative writing and an MA in geography. She has lived in many different places but enjoys writing about the small town in Western Pennsylvania where she grew up, attending a one-room school with six grades and one teacher, riding a donkey named Clementine, counting cars on the passing trains, and playing with a pet monkey. She and her husband moved to the Applegate five years ago to be near their grandchildren.

Heather Murphy, a native of Pennsylvania, has been calling the Applegate home since 1993. Heather studied literature and writing at Pennsylvania State University and currently facilitates a weekly writers' workshop at the Applegate Library that is open to the public. She is also a member of the Applegate Poets, assembled by Oregon's fifth poet laureate, Lawson Inada, that performs public readings on a regular basis. Heather resides with her family on Thompson Creek Road. Her blog is www.anothersideofjune.com, and her email address is junestar108@gmail.com.

H. Ní Aódagaín has been writing and publishing fiction, essays, and poetry for the past twenty-five years. Her writings, which explore feminism, parenting, spirituality, and land-based living, have been published both regionally and nationally. She is seeking publication of her debut novel, *If Not for the Silence*, which explores the silences we live with and how those silences frame our choices and our destiny.

Joan Peterson retired from teaching writing at Rogue Community College several years ago. She lives on her farm in the Applegate, where she has room for gardening and walking. Sometimes she even has time to write a poem. Her work has appeared in *Intricate Homeland, Voices of the Siskiyous, Oregon English Journal,* among other literary magazines. She has published one chapbook of poems, *Brilliant by the Door,* and one book of selected poems, *Looking for a Place to Write.* Joan's email address is joanpete5317@gmail.com.

Jane Robin's work is deeply spiritual and erotic, since she believes that "the loves we hold in our arms help us drop barriers and connect with source." In performance, she prefers to read her pieces between Gospel refrains. In the last three decades she has been mothering, obtaining her BA and MA, teaching public school, and writing poetry on the side. She lives "in paradise"—on a creek in Williams where birds praise her work at sunrise. Her email address is JaneR@efn.org.

Hailing from Indiana, **J.D. Rogers** moved from Los Angeles to Applegate in 1988. A lifelong "unknown rock star," J.D. was the editor of the *Applegater* for almost twenty years before returning to his musical roots and releasing a rock CD titled *Just Like You*. He is the author of *Ramblin' Rants and Doggy Tales*, a compilation of articles he wrote for the *Applegater*. He claims to have been nominated fourteen times for southeast Utah's "Deranged Lizard Award." His email address is littlemuddyred@gmail.com.

Ohio-born, **John Richard Sack** has a BA in English from Yale and an MA in creative writing from the University of Washington. He spent two years in a Trappist abbey, where Thomas Merton was his novice master. He later trained in a Hindu ashram in India. Spiritual awakening and transformation are his literary themes. His novels include *The Franciscan Conspiracy*, published in sixteen languages. His nonfiction books, *Yearning for the Father* and *Mystic Mountain*, are guides to contemplative prayer. John's email address is cyberscribe2@gmail.com.

Kirsten K. Shockey, mother, homesteader, writer, and educator, finds solace in the warmth of hand milking a cow on a frosty morning and the beauty of twisted trees along a roadway. She is passionate about helping people take responsibility for their food. She writes about sauerkraut and life, not necessarily in that order. She and her husband wrote the book *Fermented Vegetables*. Kirsten's website and blog address is fermentistas.kitchen, and her email address is kirstenshockey@gmail.com.

Christina Strelova and her husband, Craig Rasmussen, have lived in Williams, Oregon, for the past twelve years. Christina spends much of her time growing and marketing gourmet garlic, showing and caring for her Irish Wolfhounds, and drawing and sculpting. When the inspiration carries her, she writes poetry. Her email address is wolfh@oigp.net.

Barbara Summerhawk makes migratory flights between Japan and Humbug Creek Road in the Applegate, where she stargazes from meadows and occasionally dips in the river near the Applegate Store. She is the author of several books based on her work and friendships in Japan and has published many stories and poems. She is growing old disgracefully.

Marilyn Terry was born at the beginning of World War II and lived in Holland, where her mother worked with the Dutch underground resistance. Six years ago she moved to the Applegate from the San Francisco Bay Area. Art and writing have always been part of her life. She has published articles in magazines and has writings and artworks always "in progress." She writes something every day, either journal entries or short stories, which she enjoys illustrating. Marilyn's email address is marilynterryart@aol.com.

Paul Tipton, a native of Pennsylvania, has spent over forty years in the Applegate working in forests, on farms, in vineyards, and as a carpenter around the valley. He has published a few things in small printings over the years, but he enjoys poetry most when it is spoken aloud. Paul's email address is ptipton@frontier.com.

Stew Towle lives on the side of Grayback Mountain in Williams with a wonderful compound of co-creators. He performs as a poet, actor, and musician. You may have seen him spitting at the monthly Ashland Poetry Slam, playing upright bass at Cocina's open mic, or acting in Grants Pass's Barnstormers Theater. He enjoys giving away homemade stickers and zines at temporary intentional communities and currently toils on an original post-apocalyptic sci-fi series. He loves walking labyrinths. His email address is revostewtion@gmail.com, and his blog address is revostewtion.blogspot.com.

Thalia Truesdell is a weaver who has been happy to call the Applegate her home since 1988. For fifteen years before that she was happy to live on the Salmon River in northern California. She is the author of *Threads: Another Salmon River Production* and is currently branch manager at Ruch Library. Thalia's website is www.thaliaweaver.com, and her email address is thalia@thaliaweaver.com.

In **Marina Walker**'s mind, words often burst forth when a place or an event inspires her. Typically, she has to hunt around for a scrap of paper to jot her impressions down. Then the notes flutter off to who knows where! Since moving to southern Oregon in 2006, she started putting those words together into poems. It is her way of paying tribute to a memorable place. She loves to reflect on those magic moments.

Christin Lore Weber has lived in the Applegate for sixteen years. Before that she lived in Minnesota, earned masters and doctoral degrees in theological studies, and became a spiritual guide at Wisdom House, a chaplain at a treatment center for troubled children, a coordinator of religious education in the Catholic Archdiocese of Minneapolis-St. Paul, a teacher in a Catholic Academy, and a Catholic nun for fourteen years. She has published eleven books, including the award-winning *Altar Music*. Contact her at storyweaver1@gmail.com and read her blogs at:
casachiara.blogspot.com (shared with husband, John Sack)
christinloreweber.blogspot.com
christinspaces.blogspot.com
lorelands.blogspot.com.

Greeley Wells, known locally for his art shows, Christmas cards, and "Jacksonville Christmas" prints, worked on animated TV commercials in Los Angeles, even sharing in a Clio award. He is a National Endowment for the Arts grant recipient. Retiring in the late 1980s from commercial art, he moved to Oregon to paint and draw from the figure. Now a filmmaker, he recently received the Best Short Documentary award from the Columbia Gorge International Film Festival for his nature film, "Greeley's Nature." Find him at greeley@greeley.me, www.greeley.me, and www.greeleyandfriends.com.

About the Applegater

The *Applegater* newsmagazine provides all residents of the Applegate's many rural and diverse communities with a communications vehicle, free of charge. Published quarterly by Applegate Valley Community Newspaper, Inc. (AVCN), a nonprofit 501(c)(3) corporation, the *Applegater* presents constructive, relevant, educational, and entertaining reports on a wide variety of subjects such as natural resources, ecology and other science information, historical and current events, community news and opinions. All articles are contributed by community members.

AVCN encourages and publishes differing viewpoints and, through the *Applegater* newsmagazine, acts as a clearinghouse of opinions for this widespread community. AVCN is dedicated to working together with community members to maintain and enhance the quality of life that is unique to the Applegate.

The *Applegater* is funded by donations from loyal readers and advertisements. All proceeds from the sale of this book will help to continue the publication of the *Applegater*, first published in 1994.

All authors in this book donated their stories and poems in support of the *Applegater*. For that, they have our deepest appreciation.

The *Applegater* Board of Directors
www.applegater.org